Under a
Black Star

Under a Black Star

Jean Milone

iUniverse, Inc.
Bloomington

Under a Black Star

Book edited by Generosa Gina Protano and produced by iUniverse in collaboration with GGP Publishing, Inc., in Larchmont, NY 10538 (www.ggppublishing.com)

iUniverse books may be ordered through booksellers or by contacting:

iUniverse
1663 Liberty Drive
Bloomington, IN 47403
www.iuniverse.com
1-800-Authors (1-800-288-4677)

Because of the dynamic nature of the Internet, any web addresses or links contained in this book may have changed since publication and may no longer be valid. The views expressed in this work are solely those of the author and do not necessarily reflect the views of the publisher, and the publisher hereby disclaims any responsibility for them.

Any people depicted in stock imagery provided by Thinkstock are models, and such images are being used for illustrative purposes only.
Certain stock imagery © Thinkstock.

ISBN: 978-1-4620-4294-4 (sc)
ISBN: 978-1-4620-4295-1 (ebk)

Printed in the United States of America

iUniverse rev. date: 08/29/2011

Dedication

This book is dedicated to Mama for her unceasing, unselfish, unconditional love; and to my sisters Mary (Maria), Mamie (Rose), and Vicky (Vincenzina), for giving Mama all their love in return.

Editor's Note

I was working late one evening last fall when the phone rang. An older woman's quivering voice at the other end of the line asked me if I published books, and if I would publish hers. I replied that we could probably help her and asked for her name and where she was calling from. We receive many such calls from different parts of the country, but this one was very local! The call was from Mamaroneck, New York—Larchmont is one of the two villages that comprise the Town of Mamaroneck—and the lady's name was Jean Milone.

Before long Jean Milone was at the front door of the building that houses my company, GGP Publishing, Inc., accompanied by her daughter Debbie Serra. The two women were coming for an initial meeting with me to discuss Jean's "story," with a copy of Jean's manuscript *Under a Black Star* in hand. I rushed to meet them at the top of the stairs, knowing that Jean would have some difficulty climbing up, given her eighty-nine years of age. Lo and behold, Jean Milone was none other than the dignified Italian-American woman who sings in the choir at the Italian Mass at St. Vito's the first Sunday of the month. For years I had wondered why this American-born woman would be found singing with immigrant women directly from Italy, but I had never thought to ask any one. Tall and slender, always well dressed, and wearing eyeglasses—Jean had always cut a refined and elegant figure to my eyes.

We talked for a good two hours, with Jean doing most of the talking. Jean related her life story over and over again. I was touched by what she had to say and by the commitment she felt in honoring the promise she had made her dying mother sixty-six years earlier. Her story and sense of honor reminded me of the stories and sense of honor of many other Italian immigrants whom I have known and who are no longer with us—stories that have yet to be told. I agreed to read the manuscript and get back to them.

~

There are several reasons that motivated me to publish *Under a Black Star*. First, it is history: It is the history of Italian immigration to the United States and therefore, American history. It is of interest not only to Italian-Americans and Americans in general but also to Italians—especially since Italy now resembles the United States as far as immigration (both legal and illegal) is concerned. Second, it's the true story of a Sicilian family that partially transplants itself to the New York City area with Fina, the author's mother, and her misfortunes at the center. The story is narrated by her first-born child, who became a coparent for her sisters and, finally, a parent after the death of their mother. Third, it is the story of a mother's love for her children and the extent to which she would go to keep them together. Fourth, and most important, the story reads well. Narrated in a simple and rudimentary way, it captures your interest and moves you along.

As I edited the book I chose to retain the artistically naïve quality of the manuscript, which I find charming. Although I thought it fitting to make some editorial adjustments, I always kept an eye or ear to respecting the original flavor of the text.

Generosa Gina Protano
Larchmont, NY
July 19, 2011

Preface

This story is a true story. This vivacious woman had taught her four daughters how to survive from hardship in life. My three sisters and I remember how our mother sacrificed and suffered all her life for us. For a woman who had to fight since her childhood, she finally began to lose her spunk when the evil within her was taking over.

She had begun to write her life story before it was too late. Unfortunately, it was getting very difficult for her to continue what she had started. When I saw her struggling, I promised Mama that I would write her story. She had been telling us her life story time and time again from beginning to end.

This has been an extremely difficult undertaking for me since I'm not a writer. If I hadn't made the promise to write her story, I would never have attempted to do it. While writing, it brought back horrible and unpleasant memories. She was really born "Under a Black Star."

I should really give credit to my sisters for reminding me to write our mother's story as I promised I would. I'm sorry that I waited until I was eighty-nine years old to keep my promise. I was afraid and felt guilty that I would be called to my Maker never keeping my promise to Mama. I should have written this years ago; but after my three sisters and I got married, life took a turn in the road and delayed this writing. The title of this story is: *Under a Black Star*.

My mother was five years old when she was raped. They found her bleeding and unconscious in a field in her hometown in Italy. My grandfather had a dance studio with many students. When he found out that one of his students was responsible for raping his daughter, he shot him. He was exonerated because it was believed his actions were justified.

His child was looked on as "soiled" material. My mother suffered all her life because of it. She was a very happy and loving child. My grandmother ran the family grocery store, and both grandparents had a wonderful reputation and were well respected. Grandma would make my mother her lunch for school every day.

In school the children were mean to her and avoided her because their mothers told them not to play with her. Every day they would take her lunch and replace it with someone else's lunch. Mama told the teacher that someone was taking her lunch. The teacher would tell her to sit down, eat her lunch, and not cause any trouble. She wasn't pleasant, and didn't like Mama either because of what had happened.

Every day it was the same story. Finally, Mama came to know who it was. One day after school Mama went out and hid behind a tree until the girl passed by on her way home. Mama grabbed the girl, pinned her down on the ground; and while she was kicking and screaming, she cut her beautiful long, curly hair to the scalp. She cut her eyebrows and eyelashes, too. She warned the girl not to steal her lunch anymore, gave her a swift kick in the rear, and sent her home screaming.

Mama gathered all of the girl's hair and fled. She knew she was in deep trouble, and so she hid. The girl's mother dragged her crying daughter by the hand, with a big crowd following her, to my grandmother's house.

With her hands on her hips she screamed to my grandmother, "Look what your daughter did to my child!" Grandma saw the child. She looked like a devil, and Grandma almost laughed. She told the woman she was going to give Mama a good whipping when she got home. In the meantime, Mama was in the crowd unnoticed; and she went up to the woman in the midst of her rant and bit her arm hard and fled.

Mama ran into the stable, climbed the ladder into the upper loft, and pulled up the ladder. Grandma came yelling at her to come down. Of course, she couldn't go after her because Mama had pulled the ladder up after her. Grandma yelled, "Wait till your father comes home!"

When Grandpa came home and was told what had happened, he said, "Enough is enough. That child is being harassed for something that happened to her through no fault of her own. Good for her! It's about time this stop!"

Grandpa went to the stable and called out to Mama to come down. He understood what his child was going through. She came down; he hugged her, told her she'd have to fight for her rights, and gave her credit for having the spunk to fight.

Mama was happy that her father knew she was right and that she had had enough. So with all the beautiful long curls she had cut, she glued them on her doll's head. She was pleased with how pretty the doll looked. Her lunch was never taken again.

∼

Grandma and Grandpa had four girls and two boys: Agatha, Salvatore, Domenic ("Dom"), Josephine, Eleanor, and Sadie. Mama liked to cook, so she always cooked things that Grandpa liked. He liked many different foods, and she was pleased to make them. Each one of the children had chores to do.

Once Grandma asked Mama to get the chickens inside the fence. When she couldn't get them in, Mama went to the wine cellar to get a stick to make the chickens go in. While in the cellar, out of curiosity to know how each barrel of wine tasted, she sampled each one of them. Needless to say, without any food in her, she got a bit tipsy. She went out with the stick to shoo the chickens inside the fence. As she got near the chickens, she swung with all her might. With the stick, she knocked the chickens and pushed them inside the fence. She said, "Oh, you had to wait for me to hit you to go in. Maybe next time I tell you, you'll go in and stay there. She got them all in.

One day Mama's youngest brother, Dom, went to a neighbor's house. The woman was frying fish for dinner. When the family sat down to eat, they didn't offer Dom any fish. He came home and told Mama how he yearned for some of that fish. When the fish vendor came around in his fish cart, Mama ordered a basket full of fish. She cooked the fish, and made her brother have his fill.

~

A few years later Grandpa decided he wanted to come to America. Grandma wouldn't come. She was afraid of the ocean and wouldn't leave her native Sicily. So she stayed behind, and Grandpa came with his oldest daughter, Agatha, and my mother, Fina. Later on, he called for his youngest daughter, Eleanor, and his youngest son, Dom. Dom and Eleanor became excellent dancers after taking dance lessons in Grandpa's dance studio in Italy. They became partners and won many trophies.

When Dom and Eleanor arrived in New York City, the family all lived in a cold water flat. Any friends who arrived from Italy to America would come to visit Grandpa. Mama did the cooking to make dinner for them. Once, when Mama was making dinner, a mouse ran across a display dish on the shelf above the stove, slipped, and fell into the sauce. It was too late in the day to make another pot of sauce, so Mama scooped out the dead mouse and completed the meal as all the people were hungry. She didn't say anything, just cooked the spaghetti and served it with the sauce.

After supper, Mama asked her Uncle Tony how he had liked dinner. He said that it had been superb. When she told him what had happened to the sauce, he upchucked his whole dinner.

Agatha met someone, fell in love, got married, and had two boys. A few years later they decided to go back to Italy. Eleanor also got married, she married Frank. My mother met her husband, Domenic, at a family function. He was six feet two inches tall, and Mama was only four feet eight inches tall. They both fell in love. He wanted to marry her, but she said no. Mama felt no one would want to marry her once they found out that she had been raped. He told her he was aware of it, but that he still loved her and wanted to marry her. Mama was reluctant to marry him because Grandpa would object. Domenic convinced her to marry him, and they eloped. Then she found out that he was only eighteen years old, while she was twenty-two.

Grandpa was very upset. He had wanted a decent wedding for his daughter, and he wouldn't talk to either one of them for a long time. He had wanted only the best for Mama. Mama and Dad bought a house at 9743 Eighty-Fourth Street in Ozone Park, Queens, New York. A year later, Mama gave birth to a set of twin girls. They lived for six months before dying from pneumonia a week apart.

A few years later, Grandpa became sick and decided to go back to Italy and live the rest of his life there. Grandma took care of him until he died.

I was born in 1922, a year after the twins died. A year and a half later, my sister Maria was born. Then a year and a half later, Rose was born. Everyone that came to visit and saw her said she was "*bella*, like a rose"; so they decided to call her Rose.

My dad was a tailor and a snappy dresser. He owned a motorcycle with a passenger seat alongside of it. He bought a new home. Dad was envied by Uncle Frank because he couldn't afford what my dad had.

Grandma, Great Grandma, and Aunt Sadie.

Mama. Circa 1913.

Mama and Aunt Agatha.

Grandpa and Aunt Agatha.

Aunt Nancy and Uncle Domenic.

Grandma, Aunt Sadie, and Aunt Agatha.

Jean Milone

My dad loved dancing. He was so tall and my mother was so short. If she was talking to someone, Dad would ask her what the person had said. Mama was a kidder, and would tell him that they wanted to know if he was her father since he looked older than his age.

Mama knew how to sew (all the girls in the family were dressmakers), and she dressed me well. I had outgrown a dress, and Mama gave it to a neighbor for her little girl. The day the girl wore the dress, she was sitting in the street playing. It was a new development of houses, and the streets weren't paved yet. Recognizing that it was my dress, I quickly pulled the dress off her and left her crying and screaming. When I came home and showed the dress to Mama, she went and apologized to the girl's mother.

One cold winter night my parents were invited to a party with dancing. After getting overheated and perspiring from dancing, Dad decided to step outside to cool off. As a result, he got a cold and became very sick with pleurisy. He had to go to the hospital from time to time to have the fluid drained out. Then he developed tuberculosis and had to remain in the hospital. When his condition worsened and he was tired of being in the hospital, he snuck out to come home where he eventually died.

Dad was unable to work during his illness, and things were pretty tough for Mama. She went to the priest to ask for help. He put his hand in his pocket and handed her a dime. She said, "Father, with this I can only buy a quart of milk." He shrugged his shoulders and said that was all he had. Mama was a very religious woman, and she left heartbroken.

Mama went to this woman's house, a distant relative, for a cup of sugar; and because everyone in the family was afraid that tuberculosis was contagious, she wouldn't let Mama in. You couldn't blame her!

When my paternal grandmother came to visit my father, she accused Mama of making my father sick. Dad got upset with Grandma for making such accusations. I saw Mama crying; and Dad turned to Grandma and yelled, "What are you talking about? My wife has done everything for me! If she could get milk from a bird, she would!"

Then I yelled at Grandma for making Mama cry and asked her to get out of our house. Grandma felt that Mama had urged me to do that. Grandma never approved of my parent's marriage. She, too, felt that Mama was "soiled." As Grandma was leaving, yelling and screaming unpleasant words at Mama, she tripped and fell down the front steps and injured her leg.

It wasn't much longer after that incident that Mama gave birth to my sister Rose. She was born on July 4, 1925, and Dad died two months later, on September 11. The wake was held at home. I remember Mama asking me to bring the two undertakers upstairs to Mama and Dad's bedroom. My Dad was twenty-four years old, and he had had a set of twins and three more girls in his lifetime.

The day of the funeral, I was playing outside in the front yard. There was no lawn, only dirt. As I had said earlier, the house was in a new development; and the lawns were not planted yet. As I was playing, the funeral car was just getting lined up. Two women were standing in the doorway of my house. They were saying to each other, "What a shame, these children are now fatherless." There was only one limousine following the hearse.

When Dad died, Mama's trousseau and all her belongings were burned in the back yard in an open fire. Because of his tuberculosis, everything was supposed to be contagious.

After Dad's death, Mama would often cry and say, "Oh why did you leave me? Why did you leave me?" as she held Rose in her arms.

After Dad was buried, we couldn't live in our house any more; we could not pay the mortgage. Mama begged Aunt Eleanor and Uncle Frank to take over the house. They didn't have a down payment to buy their own house, so Mama suggested they assume the payments of her mortgage and change the name of the owners to theirs. In return, Mama asked that they pay her for the deposit that she and Dad had put down on the house when they could afford it. Aunt Eleanor and Uncle Frank agreed.

~

The government came. It took Maria and me away from Mama, and put us into an orphanage. Maria was one-and-a-half years old, and I was three. Mama cried and begged them not to take us away from her. They told her she couldn't support us. Mama argued that if their intention was to help her go to work so she could get her children back, then take Rose too, who was only eight weeks old, until she could get back on her feet. They refused.

From the orphanage, they moved Maria and me to foster homes. Maria's foster parents neglected her. I was treated well. Unfamiliar with the system, Mama was helpless. In order to establish the kind of home necessary for the return of her children, she was advised that she would have to remarry.

Mama was heartbroken. She got a room in a basement, left Rose in the care of a neighbor, and went to work. She wanted her children back no matter what. It ripped her heart out when she'd come home from work to see how the neighbors' children ran to their father or mother when they would come home from work. Mama cried also when she would see Aunt Eleanor's children run to Uncle Frank when he would come home from work. Mama couldn't sleep; she cried worrying about Maria and me. Although Mama was small in stature, she was grand in spirit. She was knocked down many times, but she was always able to pick herself up, shake off the dust, and start all over again. She instilled that in us, and we've followed through; but sometimes there comes a time when you become too tired of picking yourself up and you start getting into a rut, that's when things are not in focus anymore. The burden becomes too heavy to carry on your shoulders, and you weaken.

After many months, Mama went to the priest to talk to him about releasing us from the foster homes so she could have us back. Before going to the Rectory, she took one of my father's guns and a gallon of Kerosene. It was on a Friday. She went to the Rectory, rang the doorbell, and entered. She found the housekeeper very busy cooking trays of chicken. In those days we didn't eat meat on Friday. She asked Filomena, the housekeeper and cook, where the priest was. Filomena pointed her down the hall. When walking down to the door at the end of the hall, she heard the priest singing. Mama could see him walking back and forth through the stained glass window. She knocked on the door. He didn't answer, so she opened the door and stood there. The priest was walking and singing along the side of a long table beautifully set with dishes, glasses, and napkins fit for a banquet affair. When he was about to come to the corner of the table singing, "Filomena, Filomena, Filomena of my heart," he swirled and saw my mother. With an angry tone, he said to Mama, "By God! Why didn't you ring the doorbell before entering?" In Italian, Mama answered, "Who the heck saw the doorbell? I knocked." He answered, "How dare you curse in the house of God!" Mama answered, "I didn't curse or see the doorbell; I was told by Filomena to knock and walk in." Of course, he was embarrassed that Mama found him singing about the housekeeper. He then asked her what she wanted. Mama told him she wanted her children back. He told her she was crazy. Mama was very, very upset and said to him, "Yes, I am crazy because I want my children back! If I don't get them back, I have nothing. I lost my husband, my children, my house; I have nothing left. Now I have nothing to live for. I have my husband's gun with me to shoot you, and with this gallon of Kerosene I'll set the church and Rectory on fire!"

The priest tried to calm her down, telling her she couldn't have us. She threatened, "I am not fooling around, and I'll tell the Pope about your singing and having an affair with the maid. I am very serious!" The priest said, "All right, I'll make a call." She had the gun pointed at him, telling him, "Don't try to trick me because I understand English." When he got off the phone, he told her to calm down and go to the orphanage on a certain day to pick us up. Mama thanked him and left.

Mama went to the orphanage with a French woman she knew and trusted who could translate for her to make sure she was getting her children back. Mama found me sitting on the examination table with a doctor checking me before releasing me, but she didn't see Maria. Mama asked me in Italian, "Where is your sister?" I pointed to her, and Mama went to her. She didn't recognize Maria because she was malnourished. She was skin and bones with a big potbelly. Her stomach was so swollen she looked like she was pregnant. Maria's stomach had to be pumped, and she had to be put on a special diet and medication. She was so afraid and delicate, even years later.

To this day it aggravates me to think that rather than pay the foster parents, they could have given the money to my mother to support us and keep us with her.

~

Maria and I were taken care of by the same neighbor who was caring for Rose. Mama continued to work; and as soon as she could afford it, we moved from Ozone Park to New York City to a small three-room apartment in a tenement building next door to a cousin of Mama's. We used to have to put a quarter in a meter to get gas lighting from a light fixture that was mounted on the wall.

In New York City, Mama continued to work and left us children in the care of a woman. She would bring the woman our lunches, milk, and goodies. The woman was a nice lady; but when her grown nephew would come, she would put us out on the fire escape to play and feed her nephew some of our food and goodies. One day when it was sprinkling, she put us on the fire escape because her nephew was coming. I looked in the window and saw them at the kitchen table and what she was doing with our food. After her nephew left, she let us in. I guess she thought we were too young to understand. I told Mama and she told the woman not to do it anymore.

One Saturday at home my mother told me to hold Rose on my lap while sitting on the windowsill with Maria sitting alongside of me. The fire escape was behind us so there was no fear of us falling or getting hurt. Mama was going to wash the floor. She had a pot of boiling water. She sprinkled soap powder on the floor, poured some hot water on it, and started to scrub with a broom when she came across a piece of candy stuck to the floor. She picked it up and asked me to throw it in the garbage. I handed Rose to Maria to hold and took the candy from Mama's hand. As I turned, I slipped on the wet floor and landed on my back on the boiling pot of water. I remember only too well screaming. I knocked the pot over, making the floor even more slippery. I was crawling on my hands and knees when Mama grabbed me to try to tear my dress off. The next thing I knew was when I regained consciousness and the doctor was almost finished wrapping the last bit of gauze on my padded mummy body. I was covered from my neck down to my rear end. I was about five years old.

It was unbelievable how crowded the apartment was with a doctor, an ambulance nurse, friends, and Mama's cousin from next door. How happy everyone was when I came to. I was unconscious for quite a while, and no one left until I came to.

The apartment we had was above a deli and restaurant. They sent up hot soup and a tray of food for us. The doctor told my mother I was lucky that I had had a woolen dress on because wool doesn't absorb water as fast as cotton. I was pretty badly scalded, and the blisters were very large and deep. The dressings were very important to remove the water and avoid any infection. My mother made a vow that if I pulled through this (the doctor told my mother I could die if an infection set it), she would make me walk barefoot in the procession for the Feast of Mount St. Carmel, carrying a large candle of my height.

Periodically, I used to have to be taken to the hospital to change the dressing. When I would go, they would have me lie on the table on my stomach; and with a pair of scissors they would cut the gauze along each side of my body. Then with a pair of pliers they would hold one end of the gauze and yank the whole bandage off with one pull. I used to scream at the top of my lungs. They would blot all the blood and water and would prepare to redress the bandages. The dressings would be all ready with a row of measured strips of adhesive tape on a table, and alongside there would be a can with flame coming from it like a torch. They would take one strip of tape, heat it from end to end, and slap it on my raw back. My screams used to hit the ceiling. They would strap my arms and legs and continue until they had completed the lattice work of tape up, down, and across my back. They would then proceed with the gauze wrapping.

Mama couldn't take me to the hospital for the redressing because she passed out when she took me there herself the first time, so Uncle Dom's father-in-law would take me. He was a big, strapping man; he would walk to the hospital, which was about half a mile away, carrying me in his arms. He felt so bad for me, and he understood why my mother couldn't take me. Of course, I used to not want to go; but Mama kept telling me that if I didn't go, I would get an infection and die, and she would cry and miss me.

I had finally pretty much healed except for a patch of four or five inches. Mama asked me if I wanted her to change my dressing, instead; and I was glad not to have to go to the hospital. My back has no signs of the accident or scarring except for the little bit that my mother redressed.

As Mama had promised, when the day of the Feast of Mount St. Carmel arrived, she bought a tall candle as the procession was assembling. It was almost as tall as I was. As Mama prepared to take my shoes and socks off, the women who were going to march in the procession begged her not to let me walk all that way barefoot. They finally convinced her to let me wear my shoes.

~

When we lived in Ozone Park, before we moved to New York City, the insurance man that used to collect our insurance convinced my mother not to drop the policies. She didn't want anyone she didn't know to come to collect. He was a gentleman. He was such a good soul, and his family knew our family. He told Mama that he would come to New York City to collect, but not to tell anyone because that was not his territory. He used to take the train for a one-hour ride each way just to collect two dollars a month for four policies that were for five hundred dollars each. His train fare was five cents each way. When he would see my sisters and me hanging around Mama, he would have tears in his eyes.

Being a dressmaker wasn't always steady work. Things were tough. It was near Christmas, and we were not able to celebrate. So I wrote to the New York City Postmaster. Mama would dictate to me, and I wrote the best way I could. I hadn't started school yet. In a couple of days an elegantly dressed woman came to the door, and her driver brought up a barrel with all sorts of Christmas ornaments and gifts.

Years ago, spaghetti was not sold in packaged boxes. It was sold by the pound from a wooden box that held about twenty-five or more pounds. She brought a wooden box of spaghetti to us and canned foods. We were so happy. After that we were told where to go for food. We would stand on a bread line and get bread, cheese, potatoes, butter, and other items. I will never forget the bread line.

My mother wanted to get a sewing machine so that she could work from home and be with us children. She inquired, and an Italian sewing machine salesman, named Vincenzo, came. She was glad he was Italian, and explained to him that she wanted a sewing machine so that she could get work and sew at home. Her only problem was that she could not pay cash, but wanted to pay on an installment plan. He agreed.

Vincenzo hadn't been in America too long and was doing pretty well as a salesman. He was a charming and handsome man, and they fell in love and got married. It was four years after my father had died. Before she married, she warned him that she had three children. He said he was well aware of it, and still wanted to marry her. It wasn't long after that Mama became pregnant, and they were both ecstatic about it.

Jean Milone

After a few months, a big bombshell hit: the Depression. People were losing their jobs, they were jumping from buildings and rooftops; there was panic everywhere. My stepfather lost his job. He was terribly worried because he had no job with a pregnant wife and three children, all within a year of being married.

One evening while we were all in bed, he said to Mama, "We're short on milk. You had better go for a quart of milk." Mama took the milk tin can and went to the store. The milk in the store was kept in large country milk cans. Each dipper was sized to measure out a one-half quart or full quart of milk.

Upon Mama's return home, she found her husband on the floor, having hung himself from the bedpost. She screamed, and I jumped out of bed. I opened the door; and as I was going toward her, I stepped on his face. She grabbed me, picked me up, and threw me on my bed; and she closed the door.

She cut the rope from his neck and tried to revive him. Her cousins heard her screaming and came running in. They saw the situation and called the police. In no time the place was filled with police.

They retraced everything my mother was able to tell them. They measured the rope around his neck that she had cut. Then the officer opened the door to my room and found me crouched in the corner of my bed crying. He picked me up and told me everything was all right, and he covered my face so that I wouldn't see my stepfather on the floor. Two other policemen came; they each picked up one of my sisters while they were sleeping and took them out of the room.

They took us outside so we wouldn't see our stepfather's body being removed. One of the policemen asked if we wanted anything. Maria asked for a banana. In the meantime, the other policemen were investigating. Poor Mama was devastated as newspaper reporters were taking our pictures. We surrounded her clutching her as she was sitting in a chair, too weak to even hold up her head. She was expecting a baby in a few months.

Mama was crying while I had my arms around her neck. I promised her that I would take care of her when I grew up.

I kept that promise. At only thirty-three years of age, she was widowed twice.

That night, we slept at Uncle Dom's apartment, which was a few blocks away from ours. Then we moved from our apartment to one across the street from my uncle's apartment.

~

After we moved, I kept asking Mama for a doll; and she told me she would get me a real live doll if I saved my money. I didn't understand that Mama was carrying a baby. Uncle Dom's wife, Aunt Nancy, volunteered to save the money for me. She offered to put my money in her empty flowerpot in a wicker basket on a three-legged stand. So, every penny or nickel I got, I would run across the street to Aunt Nancy's and drop my coins into the basket.

The day came when Mama was due. She told me to go get my money because she would soon get my baby. It was on January 18, 1930, on an icy, cold day. I ran across the street, slipped, and went under a parked car. I was so overly excited I didn't realize how dangerous it was trying to run across a New York City street on such a wintry day.

Aunt Nancy put my money in a bag for me to carry—less than five dollars. Mama's cousin and her daughter came from Corona, Long Island. She was an elderly woman, and we called her Zia Peppina (Italian for Aunt Josephine). Zia's daughter Marianna took me to the movies. At that time, there were only silent movies, and a man played live on an organ. The movies were five or ten cents, and had subtitles.

After the movie we headed home. Marianna dropped me off at the landlord's apartment, where Maria and Rose were staying. She told me we couldn't go upstairs yet and that we would be called up when the time came. When we did go up to our apartment, Zia said to me, "Look, I'm going to go to the store to get some food. Be very quiet because Mommy is very tired, and she needs to sleep

After she left, I tiptoed into the bedroom and saw that Mama was sound asleep with a baby cradled in her arms. I went quietly, and I gently took the baby out of her arms. I was so happy to have a new baby girl in my arms. I was going into the next room when Maria put her hand on my shoulder and said, "Let me see." I said, "No! She's mine!" Maria kept insisting she wanted to see the baby, and I didn't want to let her. When we got to the saddle of the doorway, I turned slightly so that Maria couldn't see the baby. By doing that, I tripped and dropped the baby. She landed on her face, and started to cry. I got frightened and ran and hid under my bed, which was a folding cot.

Mama jumped out of bed. The baby wasn't even an hour old. She picked up the baby and after she calmed her down, Mama applied Musterole ointment, which was like Vicks. Meanwhile, I prayed that everything would be all right. When Mama had quieted the baby, she came after me. She caught my foot, but I jerked; and she lost her grip and fell back. There was a chair next to the bed, and Mama fell against the chair and injured her back.

Childbirth had never been explained to me. I knew I had paid five dollars, and she was mine! I remained under the bed until Zia came back from shopping and took care of Mama. When all had calmed down, I came out from under the bed. That baby was mine, no matter what.

∽

At our apartment in New York City, there was no backyard to play in, so we played on the sidewalk in front of the building. Maria and I were outside, and we wanted to play. We didn't have a ball so we used and empty tin can I had spotted nearby. We kept throwing it at each other. Unfortunately Maria caught the can on the open side, and it cut her finger open. All the blood frightened me, and I ran to Mama with Maria. I explained what had happened. Mama wrapped Maria's hand and brought her to the hospital for stitches. Mama warned us never to play like that again. It was so hard to play anywhere but on the sidewalk, and there were so many people going by.

While living in New York City I saw a friend of Mama's make peanut brittle. I bought some peanuts for nine cents a pound, and shelled them. I put the peanuts in a pot and poured almost half a bag of sugar in. When Mama came in and saw all that sugar in the pot, she told me to stop and asked what I was doing. I told her I had seen her friend make peanut brittle and I was making the same. Mama allowed me to, but she removed some of the sugar because she said I had put too much in. I finished making the peanut brittle, and it turned out very good. Mama loved it. Of course, I had to clean up my mess. Mama taught us to be very clean when washing the dishes and utensils, and to scrub the pots shining clean. Otherwise, any fellow that wanted to marry us would change his mind, she would tell us. Of course, we believed everything Mama told us.

One day, I was playing in front of the tenement building as usual, while pedestrians passed by. A man dressed kind of raggedly and a little sloppily approached me and asked if I'd like some candy. I answered, "Yes." He said, "Follow me." I did, and we walked into the dark hallway of the building. It was pretty dark. He headed towards the back of the stairway that leads to the basement. Evidently, he must have unzipped the zipper of his pants. As we got to the back of the stairway, he turned around and his penis was out. He quickly grabbed my hand and placed it on his penis. I got frightened and quickly ran away. By the time I told Mama, he was gone. That's when she told us to never, ever let anyone pick up our dress and pull down our panties or touch any part of our body, even if it was our own father. I never told this to anyone until now except Mama.

Living in New York City, we couldn't afford to go anywhere. So Mama got me the cutest kitten I ever saw. I loved that kitten. The tenement apartments were cold-water flats. Each of the floors had one bathroom at the end of the hall and the four families on each floor had to share it. There was only a toilet, with no basin in which to wash. I went to the toilet one morning, and I placed my hand on the doorknob, and I opened the door. As I did, I noticed I had excrement on my hand. It was disgusting. As I looked up, I saw my kitten high on the windowsill steaming. It was dead. Someone had cooked it.

I screamed, and Mama came running out. She screamed, too. The neighbors on the same floor opened their doors to see what all the yelling was about. Our next-door neighbor also opened her door. She had a white nightgown on, and the nightgown was soiled with excrement. She kept yelling, "I'm not crazy!" My mother pulled me in and closed the door. Someone must have made a call, and she was taken away in a paddy wagon, never to be seen again. Until this day I won't have a kitten.

My poor mother couldn't always keep us busy in the apartment. When it was too much for her, she'd let me go outside unsupervised, but warned me to be very careful about everything. She couldn't come out with my younger sisters because she worked at home sewing dresses. I was busy skipping once when a large dog jumped on me and pinned me down. With my screaming, people managed to get the dog off me. Frightened and in tears, I ran into one of the tenement buildings screaming. Mama was told, and everyone was out looking for me. They finally found me; but every time I would see a dog, I would get hysterical. I would get sick from fear. To have me overcome the fear, people told Mama to get me a puppy. So Mama got me a puppy, and until I was married, I always had a dog.

~

After a few years, Uncle Dom moved away from across the street from us. He went to live in Ozone Park, Woodhaven, to open a shoe repair store on 101st Avenue and Woodhaven Boulevard and Cross Bay Boulevard. Uncle Dom was an excellent shoemaker. He had made shoes for Mama when they lived in Italy. After some time, Mama also decided to move to Ozone Park. We moved a short distance away from Uncle Dom, and a short distance away on the other side of us was

Aunt Eleanor and Uncle Frank. We were all so happy to be living near Mama's brother and sister.

Mama's oldest sister, Agatha, returned to her hometown in Sicily with her husband and two American-born sons. Mama's brother Sal and sister Sadie had never left Italy, they still lived there. Uncle Sal had five children, and Aunt Sadie lived with Grandma; she married very late in life, after Grandma died at age ninety-two.

Mama kept close correspondence with all of her family in Italy. Some years later, Aunt Agatha's husband became ill. Aunt Agatha would write letters to Mama crying. Mama couldn't see anyone suffer, knowing what she herself had gone through and was still going through.

As hard as it was for Mama, she was forever mailing Aunt Agatha packages full of stuff—coffee, food items, clothing, gifts, and whatnot. Her youngest son, Michael, wanted to be a priest, so Mama sent everything he needed to make his clothes. Her daughter, Antoinette, was in the convent. She was taken good care of, but Mama still sent her all kinds of fabrics and embroidery. Antoinette did fine hand sewing. Mama worked very hard, but she felt that if we were fed and clothed, then she should help her sister in whatever way she could. Mama would take bundles of dresses from the factory to work on at home as many hours as she could. She understood only too well what it means to be in need of help.

When Uncle Frank saw Mama with packages in the baby carriage to take to the post office, he would say to her, "Are you crazy? Agatha has a husband and boys who work and can help her. You're a widow with children. Think of your children!" But Mama continued to do it no matter what anyone said. Agatha was her sister, and she needed help.

Mama went begging with us by her side, stopping cars on the Boulevard. We also begged at a church on the corner of our street. Aunt Eleanor heard about it and was embarrassed, and she told Mama not to do it again. Aunt Eleanor also sent Agatha money without Uncle Frank's knowledge. Mama would take away from us to send it to them. Later on in life I was a little annoyed at Aunt Agatha. Did she think we picked up money by the shovelful?

When Mama had work to do at home, she did it when the storekeeper downstairs would close up and go home. Then she would start to use the sewing machine. There was a hole under the kitchen sink where our next-door neighbor would look through to see what my mother was doing. Mama became aware of it, and she put something to block the hole. She also put a skirt around the sink.

In that apartment we had a black-coal stove, and we also cooked on it. One morning, Mama went to bring the finished dresses back to the factory, and I was supposed to go to school. I decided the kitchen floor needed washing because of the shoveling of the coal. So with a pail of soapy water I started to wash the floor.

While washing, I heard a knock at the door. It was a girl who came to call me for school. I told her I had to wash the floor, and she left. Of course, she told the teacher. It took me quite a while to mop all the soapy water off the floor. I wanted so much to surprise Mama. A short time later, there was another knock at the door. Upon opening the door there stood the school truant officer saying I had to go to school. In the meantime, Mama came home. She saw the truant officer, and she asked me what I was doing home. I told her I wanted to surprise her. Instead, she was surprised by the truant officer. He took me back to school, and Mama had to finish mopping up all the water that was still on the floor.

We lived across the street from a chicken market. Around the corner was an apartment above a garage that the chicken market owner also owned. Mama found out that it was for rent and that it had heat. It was a flight up to get to the apartment but that was fine with Mama. So we moved.

Mama continued to get bundles of dresses to work on, and she didn't have to worry about who was beneath us now. So she would work until late at night. The sewing machine faced a window that opened unto the roof. We could step out of the window onto the roof and hang our washed clothes. In the morning, I would make coffee in the percolator and would prepare lunches for my sisters and myself. Mama would start to work on the sewing machine early in the morning. I would give each of my sisters a wide cup, and they would break up bits of Sicilian bread to put in their coffee. That was breakfast. We had no cereal then. I used to use milk because I didn't like coffee. Mama used to say I would have to learn to drink coffee or tea because when we went visiting, it would not be right to ask for milk because people had children, too; and milk was too expensive. So I learned to drink tea, and I would make it for myself at home.

While Mama would be sewing on the dresses, she would tell me stories as I turned the dress belts inside out. I did the same for the sleeves or whatever else had to be done. She would tell me the story slowly in dribs and drabs, not to finish the story too soon. She also kept adding to the story to keep it interesting so that I would stay awake and keep her company.

The chicken market lady had prize pigeons in the coop on the roof. Many times men would climb up a ladder crouching to get to the prize pigeons and steal them. Mama was afraid. What if they saw her through the window and came after her? So she would yell, "Get the gun, there are crooks trying to steal the pigeons!" and they would take off.

~

At school I was liked. I had a very good singing voice, and I was always picked for lead parts. I loved to sing. Mama knew words to the opera, but she couldn't sing and couldn't teach me. One day, my school principal came to our home with a middle-aged couple to talk to Mama about me. They wanted to take me to La Scala, in Milan, Italy, to get training as an opera singer and be their prodigy. But I wasn't to get in touch with anyone at home because they feared that if something happened in the family, it might affect my voice and performance. Of course, I was thrilled because I wanted so much to be a singer; but Mama said no. I was terribly disappointed. Mama knew how much I loved to sing and she could see I was so disheartened. Then she explained that it would be a long trip by boat; I wouldn't have any contact with my family; and that as much as Italy loves music and their singers, the singer had to submit to the one who hired her in order to get the job. She said, "Wait until you become a mother, then you'll see if you would let your child go with strangers." Hearing her reasoning and knowing how she sacrificed all her life for her children, I realized that I couldn't leave Mama. They left disappointed, but understood.

How well I remember this incident. It's one I'll never forget. Once, my cousin Margie came to our house to have dinner with us. Mama made spaghetti and sauce. When she dished it out, Margie took her dish and went to eat at the window. Mama noticed, but didn't say anything, figuring she'd come back to the table when she'd see we were all sitting at the table. Rose knew that Mama didn't allow us to leave the table with food; but being the daring type, although she knew that she could get into trouble, she left the table to sit by the window with Margie, anyway. Mama was so frustrated. She rarely got angry; but when she did, she made up for all the times she hadn't. She took Rose's dish and slapped it on her head. The dish broke, and the spaghetti came streaming down her face. Rose never said a word; she just slurped the spaghetti that hung in front of her face. When Margie saw what happened, she immediately took her dish and went back to the table without a word. Actually, all Mama had to do was to clear her throat, and that was a signal for any of us to be careful. I guess this time she was beside herself.

When Mama had to work at the shop, our baby sister, Vincenzina, named after her father Vincenzo, would be left with a babysitter who lived next door to Aunt Eleanor's. When I would come home from school with Maria and Rose, I would get some snacks and drinks, then go pick up Vincenzina, put her in the carriage, and take them all to Forest Park. There was a lovely playground there with swings, slides, and other play equipment. You could have picnics as there were tables, benches, and outdoor grills. We used to have to be home before dark. When Maria would get tired from the long walk, she'd get a chance to sit at the bottom of the carriage; and Rose and I would push the carriage.

I was a very responsible child, and had a key to the apartment. I was like a little mama. I would get home from the park before it got dark and prepare food for supper. I would open up a can of tomato paste, chop up some garlic, put oil in a pot, and add the garlic. Just before the garlic got golden brown, I would put in the tomato paste and add a can of water. I added salt, pepper, and fresh basil; and would let it cook. Then I would put up a large pot with water so when Mama came home, I would heat the water and cook the spaghetti.

We had a small railroad apartment. In the so-called railroad apartments all rooms of each apartment were in a row on either side of a long hallway and windows were only on the front and back of the buildings. The windows in the back of our apartment opened onto the flat roof of the garage, all we had to do was step over the windowsill to step onto it. We would hang our washed clothes on a line; and on hot days when it rained, Mama would let us put on our bathing suits and go out onto the roof to cool off.

We had no friends on the block and there were no children; so when Mama used to go to see Aunt Eleanor, we were happy to go because we could play with Margie and her twin brother, Frankie. They were nine months younger than I was. Aunt Eleanor did have two other children, but they had both died before they were three.

Aunt Eleanor used to tell me that when I was a toddler and Mama went to see her, she couldn't understand why the twins would be crying, although she had fed them. Then one time she found me hiding and drinking the babies' bottles. The mystery was solved, and Mama gave me my own bottle. As we got older, we loved playing with the twins.

One evening, Mama had something to bring to Aunt Eleanor, and we went with her. When we got there, Rose ran ahead, knocked on the door, opened the door, and went down to the kitchen. They lived in the one-family house that used to be ours but that had been converted into a two-family house. The kitchen was in the basement. It was nicely built with cabinets all around the room. Maria and I followed Rose down the stairs. As my mother was coming down the stairs, she heard Uncle Frank remark in disgust, "What, the whole regime came?" Uncle Frank was standing at the table about to cut a steak. Mama noticed that Rose had removed her coat. Out of frustration, like lightning Mama slapped her face hard and said to her, "Who told you to take your coat off?" She turned around and said to Uncle Frank, "I only stopped by to drop off this package."

We went up the steps and out the door and headed for home. All of us were hanging on Mama while she was crying and so were we. Rose knew that Mama didn't mean to hit her. Mama rarely hit us. When we got home, she put us to bed, and went into the kitchen and turned all the gas jets on. She had had it. It seemed every time she did something good, she would be knocked down for one reason or another. She had had enough of life. She felt she was always looked down upon.

Aunt Eleanor had gotten very angry at Uncle Frank for his outburst, and she had argued with him. She loved Mama, no matter what faults she may have had. She came to our apartment alone. When she knocked and didn't get an answer, and smelled gas, she called the janitor to open the door. They turned off the gas jets and opened the windows. We were all revived from sleep. Aunt Eleanor had saved our lives.

Aunt Eleanor felt terrible, and apologized for Uncle Frank's thoughtless behavior. She told Mama not to pay attention to him. He was sarcastic most of the time. Aunt Eleanor had such compassion for Mama knowing how she struggled through life and how she strived to keep her head above water.

I wanted so much to help Mama that one day I filled the bathtub with hot water and emptied all the clothes from the laundry bag into the bathtub. I didn't know not to put the black stockings and all the black clothes in together with the lighter clothes. I got the washboard and got on my knees to scrub the clothes as best I could. Of course, the black clothes in the hot water ran through to the lighter clothes. I then squeezed out the soapy water and rinsed them with cold water and hung them on the rooftop clothesline to dry. Mama knew I was trying to be helpful even though I had ruined the clothes. She said although she appreciated my efforts, I should never put black clothes with the lighter clothes.

By the age of nine I had learned a lot. I was already able to use the factory Singer sewing machine and help Mama. Mama would come home with a bundle of dresses to sew. She would sew most of the dresses in a bundle. Although I was able to complete a dress, I could not sew with speed. Mama would let me run the seams on the dresses and sew other parts of the dresses, too. We would work until late at night. I stayed up to turn the belts inside out, and she would tell me stories. Because I was going to bed late, I would sometimes doze off at my desk in school. Mama would say if I was asked what time I went to bed at night, I should answer seven thirty or eight o'clock, and that I drank a big glass of milk before bed. Mama was afraid they would take us away again.

One of my teachers called me from my desk one day and handed me a pair of shoes. I didn't know why, but she told me to put them on. I told her they didn't fit and that they hurt my feet. She scolded me saying, "Why don't they fit? Is it because you want new shoes?" I told her no, but she insisted I wear them.

By the time I got home from school, Mama noticed how I was walking and she asked me what the problem was. When I told her, she said, "All right, take them off." My mother spoke to us in Italian. She was concerned that we would forget the language. The next day, my mother took me to school. She spoke very little English, but she made herself understood. When she approached the teacher, she said to her, "Dida my daughter aska you for shoes? She na aska ya, so whya you force her to puta shoe on?" The teacher tried to explain to Mama that I needed shoes. I had shoes with holes in the soles and newspaper to cover the holes.

Mama went to the principal and told him that the teacher had forced me to wear a pair of tight shoes that neither she nor

I had asked for. He agreed with her and took her to the teachers lounge. They were having lunch. Everyone took to my mother. They were genuine and sincere in liking her; and they offered her coffee, and she accepted.

In Ozone Park, when I was about eight years old, I went to Public School 64. It was hard for me in school because I was Italian and they made fun of me; so when I would get home I would speak English to my mother. Mama turned and said to me in Italian, "Don't you ever be ashamed of your heritage. You know two languages, and they only know one. When you're in school, you speak English; but when you're home, you speak Italian. I don't want you to say to me, 'Ma, get me the big pentola,' meaning big pot." At home we actually spoke in a Sicilian dialect.

~

Maria's godparents owned a beauty parlor. Mama wanted to get a permanent. When she went inside the beauty parlor, I stayed outside to play with my cousin Sam. Uncle Dom's shoe-repair shop was right next door. After playing a while I went in to see Mama. She had a sheet across her body up to her neck. All these things were attached to her head, and there were wires extending up to a pole. I thought she was being electrocuted. I began to scream and cry in horror and tried to pull the wires off her head. Mama smiled and told me it was all right. They had to hold me back while they explained that this was the way permanents were done. They all laughed and told me not to worry, that Mama's hair was going to be curly. I was about nine years old at the time.

Mama would sometimes go to the chicken market and get chicken feet, gizzards, and intestines. We would cut the nails off and peel the skin off the feet, clean the neck, open the gizzards and cut open the intestine, wash them and then put salt on them and rub them thoroughly, rinse and cook. Mama would put other ingredients in such as parsley, celery, carrots, and tomatoes, and make delicious chicken soup; and she would put pastina in, and we had a healthy and delicious meal.

Years ago, chicken markets not only sold live chickens but also live rabbits, ducks, and turkeys. If you wanted a chicken, you would tell the butcher about what weight chicken you wanted. He would then pick one, tie its feet, and weigh it on a hook scale. Then he would pull its neck, hold on to its feet, and stick it in a hot boiling water tank. Then he would hook the tied feet on another hook over a barrel and pluck the chicken clean. If you didn't want the head, neck, gizzards and intestines, you would tell him; and he would gut it out for you. Instead of throwing the unwanted parts into the garbage waste, the butcher saved them for Mama.

About a week before Thanksgiving, Mama took us to the chicken market with the intention of buying a live turkey for Thanksgiving. I remember so well how we all wanted to hold the live turkey, but I won out. I was the oldest, so I got to carry it. I was proudly holding the turkey under my arm when the butcher convinced Mama that it wasn't the wisest thing to keep the turkey, and then cook it for Thanksgiving. It would be like killing a pet and then eating it. It would leave us with a sad impression.

Mama was convinced and so was I. Holding the turkey under my arm for a while had satisfied my need to hold it. Then with a gleam in my eyes for that achievement I happily put my cold hands in my pocket, into a very warm mess. The turkey had defecated right into my open pocket. I pulled my messy hand out and scowled, looking at my mess. My sisters' laughter was well deserved, and it served me right.

Mama did everything for us to the best of her ability. She even cut our hair. One day, while cutting Maria's hair, somehow the scissors slipped; and she cut too high in the back. She couldn't leave it looking that way, so she cut up to the highest point of the accidental cut. Then she had to shave the back up to the highest point of the cut. I believe she started the "bowl-cut" hairstyle. Well, when I saw Maria's haircut, I cried. I thought she looked ugly, and cried some more. Mama felt bad. She realized she had made a mistake, so she put a ribbon two-to-three inches wide, with a bow on top, around her head to cover up the shaved part. She also bought her an ice cream cone. Poor Maria never said a word; she was such a quiet and meek girl.

When Maria was in school, children would tease or annoy her because she was Italian. Rose was the spunky one of us; and although she was younger than Maria, she was bigger and protected her all the time. However, when they were home, Rose was the one who bothered Maria the most and teased her to the point of tears.

At times, Maria and Rose would argue, and they would hit one another until one day Mama finally said "Enough! I'm going to take Maria back to the orphanage." Mama left the house with Maria, and Rose was happy to see her go. Later in the day, when Mama came home alone, she said to Rose, "Are you happy now that your sister is gone?" By this time, Rose was sorry that she had argued with Maria. I knew Mama hadn't taken Maria to the orphanage. Her children were her life to her, and we were all she had. Mama had taken Maria to Aunt Eleanor's house. Rose saw that Mama was not sad when she came home, so she went to check in the hallway and found Maria hiding in the corner. She was happy that Maria hadn't been taken to the home.

Vincenzina was too young to understand what was going on. She was so beautiful; I loved her so much that I wanted to squeeze her hard and bite her. Instead of biting her, I would put my mouth to her arm and suck it, which would leave a purple mark on her arm. My mother couldn't imagine what the marks were from until she saw me do it. Then she slapped my mouth and said not to do it again. Vincenzina would follow me everywhere.

Mama would go to work; and when Vincenzina needed to be cleaned up, I would put her in the tub of cold water and scrub her clean. I don't know how she didn't get sick. To get hot water, we had to light the boiler, and I wasn't able to do that. But I did take good care of my sisters.

When Mama had to go somewhere, she would take Maria and Rose with her. Whenever they went out with Mama, the girls would argue which side of Mama's arm they wanted to hold. They'd be coming down the outdoor transit train steps each holding her arm. Since they were both taller than Mama, as they would hold her tightly, they elevated her and her feet did not touch the train steps or ground. Mama would keep saying, "Put me down, put me down." When it was time to cross the street, Rose daringly would pull Mama to cross. Maria, on the other hand, was afraid to cross; and she would hold Mama back until there were no cars on the road. Poor Mama used to be pulled back and forth until she would get very angry and yell at both of them to let her go. We loved Mama so much that in not wishing her any harm, we became overprotective of her.

After a few years, we moved from the apartment above the garage to a corner apartment above a drugstore on the same block where Aunt Eleanor lived (our old house). On the corner across the street was the grocery store, and at the end of the block was the butcher store. In between, there was a dry cleaner, a candy store, and a fruit and vegetable market. Across from the butcher, was a nice playground that was on the property of the public school that we attended.

Mama was known and highly respected by all the storekeepers on the avenue. We used to shop in their stores when we lived above the garage apartment.

Before we moved, Aunt Eleanor told Mama about an opening at Joseph's, a dress manufacturer in New York City that she knew of. So Mama and a friend of hers went to work there. Before Mama went to work, she would tell us if there was anything we needed, to go to the store and get it and to let the storekeeper know that she would pay them when she got home. We had a pantry room with an icebox. Although the icebox used to be filled with food, you couldn't put too much in it because it was too small.

We were living much better now. We were able to go to the movies almost every Saturday. We'd go see the Flash Gordon series or Tarzan. Children were allowed in the theater without parents. The theater had ushers who monitored the children and controlled any misbehavior. It was very nice then.

Each time Aunt Eleanor and Uncle Frank were going to go to a place of enjoyment with their children, they would alternate taking one of us to go along with them, and each time the three of us who stayed behind would cry. It would upset Mama to see her children cry.

If Mama wanted to go to my father's grave, she would ask Uncle Frank to take us to the cemetery. He always seemed a little reluctant, but she assured him that she'd pay for the gas, which she did. This one time, when Uncle Frank took us all to the cemetery, I got out of the car and slammed the door shut. As I turned, I saw that in attempting to get out of the car after me, Maria had placed her hand outside the car door to boost herself out and that the door had slammed shut on her fingers. God, I was sure her fingers were severed or broken. Maria screamed at the top of her lungs. Thank God her fingers remained intact. Every time I think of it, my stomach gets squeamish. Of course, her hand had to be taken care of. She was such a delicate child. It would have been painful whether you were delicate or not.

One night, it was getting dark and Rose was going to Aunt Eleanor's when two men attempted to grab her. She was about nine years old. She escaped from them; ran to Aunt Eleanor's house, opened the door and slammed it shut. The tenant upstairs was coming down and saw how frightened Rose was and also saw the two men at the door who took off. The tenant asked Rose what had happened.

When we first heard Rose's story, we didn't believe her. Rose was a prankster, and we thought she was telling us a tall tale. Later, two policemen came to question Rose at home. We figured that the tenant must have called the police. The police did find an abandoned car with things in it that led the police to believe it belonged to the two men. They warned us to be on our guard.

Things that happened seemed unbelievable. Once, while Rose was in her classroom, she had to go to the bathroom. She kept waving her hand to get the teacher's attention, but the teacher kept telling her to put her hands down. Finally,

Rose couldn't hold it anymore; she got up and went to the back of the room, pulled down her panties and had a bowel movement. The teacher was shocked and horrified and sent her to the principal. The principal sent a maintenance man to clean up the mess and sent someone to Mama to bring Rose some clothes. Mama was pretty upset. She told the principal in her broken English, "what kinda school isa this?" and continued to question what they expected children to do if they had to go to the bathroom and the teacher wouldn't let them. The principal agreed with Mama and reprimanded the teacher for not using better judgment.

Don't think that Mama would agree with us for anything we'd complain about. If the teacher said something that was for our benefit and we didn't do it, we'd be punished by not being allowed to go to the movies.

We really were good kids. Mama was always telling us stories of good people who helped even those that weren't so nice. She taught us to be kind, helpful, polite, considerate of others, and to work hard. She was a loving person and taught us to be the same. Of course, she also reminded us to pray to the Lord and ask the Lord to help us, too. She also told us time and time again that when you're knocked down by adversity, get up, shake the dust off, and start all over again. God knows, she tried to do just that. She was a fighter; but sometimes she got tired of falling and hitting the ground hard.

Once, in trying to emulate my mother's kind qualities, my politeness was not so appreciated. The neighbor across the street came out of her apartment building, and Mama greeted her by her first name and said good morning. I repeated her greeting "Good Morning, Angela." Abruptly, my mother slapped my mouth and said in Italian, "Did you go to school with Mrs. Gordon?" I apologized and greeted her as Mrs. Gordon. That taught me whom I can call by their first names and whom not. Mama was very kind and caring to everyone and always tried to help wherever it was needed.

I was born on Palm Sunday. I was always told that we couldn't celebrate my birthday because it was a sad time—Jesus Christ's death! Mama would cover all the mirrors in the apartment. One time, I asked Mama for a "store-bought" birthday cake like other children got with all the icing on top. But Mama said she couldn't afford to buy a birthday cake from the store at that time. Aunt Eleanor and Uncle Frank were my godparents. Aunt Eleanor felt bad for me, so she baked me a cake. I tried not to mind that it wasn't a "bought" cake or that it didn't have icing on it. But when she put stick matches for candles, that upset me; and I knocked the cake off the table and broke it. I was so hurt that everybody got a "bought" cake and I couldn't have one. Later on, Mama got me a beautiful coach carriage for my doll. The doll had curly hair and looked like Shirley Temple (that was before Shirley Temple became known). She was about two feet tall and could stand. Mama would say that it would be a shame for a girl my age to go outside to play with such a big doll. She finally convinced me that it would be nice to send it to my poor cousin in Italy. She was in a convent and didn't have anything to play with. I didn't realize it at the time, but we were poor too. So, I never played with the doll. It was gone before I got attached to it. I used the carriage to put Vincenzina in it. I never went out with the carriage either.

Sometimes, when it was my birthday, Aunt Eleanor would give me a gift whenever she saw me, even if we were outside or crossing the street. It hurt me, and I asked her, "Why don't you bring it to me at home?" She told me because she didn't have the time and she didn't want to miss my birthday. The real reason was she didn't want Uncle Frank to know what she was doing for me or for my family.

We usually had Easter with Aunt Eleanor and her family. This time, Mama bought Aunt Eleanor a live goat before Easter so she could have goat's milk. Mama loved her sister, and my Aunt loved my mother. Mama always felt her baby sister was a delicate, weak person.

When the time came to slaughter and skin the goat, a distant relative came to help Uncle Frank to skin it. Neither one of them had any experience or knowledge of how to butcher a goat. They tied the goat's hind feet and hung it on a hook from one of the wooden ceiling basement beams. They put a large basin under the goat's head to catch the blood. They stuck a sharp knife into the goat's neck thinking it would kill her. The animal kept crying "Maahaa, Maahaa, Maahaa, Maahaa" all the while they were trying to cut the fur around its neck. When it was finally slaughtered, they cooked it and served it for dinner. The kids kept looking at it and saying "Maahaa, Maahaa, Maahaa, Maahaa" and wouldn't eat any part of it. We ate everything that was being served except the goat.

Uncle Dom moved his shoemaker store closer to the vicinity of Aunt Eleanor's house. He also bought a house on the same block as Aunt Eleanor's. In fact, he bought the house that was attached to the house of a next-door neighbor of Aunt Eleanor's. Uncle Dom and Aunt Nancy had four boys who were younger than my sisters and me. They were very protective of us girls. We always wanted to go to Aunt Eleanor's because the twins were closer to our age. Besides, they had a radio to listen to stories and music. However, Uncle Frank couldn't tolerate having four more children in the house. So, Mama got us a Philco radio, something that pleased us very much, and we'd listen to *Inner Sanctum*, *The Shadow Knows*, etc., etc.

We were good kids. Mama never stopped preaching to us to watch our behavior and to always be good and kind. She was always concerned about people who loved to gossip about widowed or even divorced women. Men used to pass the time hanging out around the corner grocery store across the street from our apartment watching to see who entered our building or anyone else's home on the block. They'd watch to see how long the insurance man or anyone else who came to our apartment stayed, ready for the opportunity to accuse and gossip about them. The men never said anything about the grocery store owner who was having an affair with one of the neighbors' wife. He had a lovely wife, and she wasn't aware of the affair. Yet, he had the nerve to gossip along with the other men.

My mother was well respected. They couldn't gossip about her because she was never alone. She always had one of her children with her at all times wherever she went except when she went to work. If she went to visit a neighbor, we knew where she was. Even our dog would follow her and sit behind the door of whomever she visited. Our apartment was on the corner; so we were able to see the avenue from the front windows, and on the side window we were able to see the side street. We would wait at the front window watching for Mama to come home from work. The minute we saw her turn the corner after getting off the train two blocks away, Rose would go out and run to meet her. Of course, when she came in we'd all jump around her with hugs and kisses.

Many times, Mama would get angry when her family wouldn't come to visit us, including Uncle Dom. He would say, "What can I do? There's no man in the house." That went on for years. She would get angry and say, "If a man comes for my hand in marriage, I'll marry him, even if he has one leg. Then maybe they'll have more respect for me." She felt she was always being ignored. My mother was still young. She was in her late thirties. She thought that if she remarried, she would have more respect and a better life. Then there would be no excuses for them not to come and visit her because there was no man in the house.

Vincenzina's babysitter was also a friend of Mama's. She would climb the stairs to our apartment to come to see Mama or to tell her about her woes. During one of Mama's pregnancies, her teeth had gotten pyorrhea; so they were extracted and replaced with false teeth. When she first came home from the dentist with her false teeth, we were a little leery about going to kiss her. But my cousin Margie went right up to Mama and kissed her. That helped to put us a little at ease, and we all went up to kiss her too.

Once, the babysitter came up the steps in tears wanting to talk to Mama. As we were looking over the banister, she said she couldn't talk freely about her family because her youngest son, Robbie, was following her and would be able to overhear her conversation. Robbie was a sweet boy of Vincenzina's age, and they were playmates. Since Mama could see that her friend was upset, Mama called, "Robby!" while he was climbing up the steps behind his mother. He looked up at Mama. She opened her mouth and made her top teeth drop to the bottom teeth. Robbie was so frightened that he almost fell backward and ran home. It really was funny, and it enabled the babysitter to talk to Mama freely about her problems—as if Mama didn't have problems of her own.

The twins' birthday was on December 25. They invited all their friends except Robby. He lived next door to Aunt Eleanor's house. Robby was crying because he wanted to go to the party but wasn't invited because he didn't have a present for them. Mama knew of the situation; so she had an empty box, filled it with cut newspaper, wrapped the box up, put a ribbon on it, and gave it to Robby to bring to the twins' party. Mama said, "Robby, you go to the party; and when they start to open the gifts, you come home right away." And that's just what Robbie did. Of course, the twins were disappointed when they opened his gift. Aunt Eleanor explained to them that they were not very nice to leave Robby out just because his mother couldn't afford a gift. She said "Don't you think you hurt Robby's feelings? You play with him, and then you don't invite him to your party. And you shouldn't say anything about what he brought you to make him feel any worse. You both deserved it." They listened to her; and after the party they all went out to play, including Robby, and all was forgotten. Naturally, Aunt Eleanor knew what Mama had done. She told her before the party started.

I'm getting ahead of my story. Vincenzina wanted to go to school with Rose, and Rose took her to school. She really wasn't dressed for school. She was put in kindergarten, without Mama knowing or without her permission. Mama looked all over for her. Finally, she thought of Rose; and she went to the school. She found Vincenzina in kindergarten. Maria and I were in school and were not aware of all of this. That's when Vincenzina found out that her last name was different from ours. How sorry I am that Mama didn't think of changing her last name so it would be the same as ours. I really don't know if it was allowed years ago, or Mama didn't know about it.

Jean Milone

When Vincenzina told me nearly sixty years later that deep down in her heart she had felt different because of her last name, I was shocked. She had never questioned it or showed any discomfort because of it. We never used the term half sister. Actually, we never thought we were half sisters. I explained to her that we have the same mother but a different father. There is no difference between us because Mama carried her the same way she carried us in her stomach.

I feel she belongs to me. I love her so much. When she was born, she was such a beautiful child. Her hair was nine inches long, black and wavy. After all, she was mine; I bought her for five dollars. When I think of it, I really don't think I ever saved up that much money, but I keep telling her to this day that I paid five dollars for her and so she's mine.

As children, we always thought the storks brought the babies when you were ready to buy them. As for mothers being pregnant, we only knew that they got fat. Of course, I understood later that I hadn't really bought Vincenzina. I was not quite eight years old when she was born. As she got older, although we were both still very young, when I wasn't pleased with Vincenzina's response to what I asked her to do, I'd tell her she wasn't worth the five dollars I had paid for her. Often she'd reply crying, "I'll give you the five dollars back when I get it!"

Now as a grown-up when we reminisce, Vincenzina laughs and says, "I'll give you ten dollars back." My sisters always recognized that I gave up my childhood life to care for my family. As strict as I was with them, even at that young age, they all respected me and looked up to me as if I was their mother. Since Mama died, I get Mother's Day cards from all my sisters. They're all beautiful cards, but the ones from Vincenzina are special.

Under a Black Star

In the morning going to work in New York City, Mama and her friend would meet at the bottom of the L train station; they would then go upstairs and take the train together. They both worked at the same place. When going to work, they'd see this man standing at the bottom of the transit steps every morning as if waiting for someone. It was natural to say good morning to one another. Sometimes, Mama's friend would be late; and while Mama would be waiting, the man would converse with her. While talking, he found out a lot about my mother, and that she was a widow with four children. Actually, he knew a lot about her even before she told him.

Down at the end of our block was a midwife who had five children of her own. The midwife knew this man, Leo. He was a widower and had two stepchildren. All the time he used to stand at the bottom of the transit steps, he would actually be waiting for my mother and no one else. This midwife kept talking to Mama telling her that Leo was a good man who had had very bad luck. She told Mama that his first wife had died. Then he had married his second wife who was a widow with two daughters. He'd bring his pay to her and slip it in her bra. What the midwife didn't tell Mama was what had happened to his second wife. It wasn't until years later that Mama learned what had happened to her. During an argument, while she was pregnant with his child, Leo slapped her; and she fell down a flight of stairs. After he pushed her and she fell down the steps, the doctor came. He told Leo that his wife might lose the baby. He, in turn, asked the doctor for the receipt. The doctor got upset and said to him, "You're more concerned about the bill than your wife's condition. I should call the police." When the time came to deliver the baby, the midwife was called. She delivered a stillborn baby as a result of the fall, and Leo's second wife died shortly thereafter. After she died, Papa told the midwife he would pay her fifty dollars if she could get a nice woman for him. Mama didn't know that. Eventually, Leo proposed to Mama; but Mama said that she couldn't marry anyone because I would run away and that that was my intention if she did.

Jean Milone

One Saturday morning there was a knock on the door. I went to answer it, and there stood a man with his eyes bulging out. He seemed a little frightening; he asked for Mama, and I called her. Mama came to the door. She was rather surprised to see him. She asked him to come in. Mama turned to me and said in Italian, "This is the man who wants to marry me." He had actually come to convince me not to run away if they got married.

Leo told me we could listen to the radio, go to the movies, and have other privileges. What he was telling me wasn't making any sense to me. We were already doing the things he was promising he would allow us to do. We already listened to the radio, and on Saturday's we'd go to the movies. So, he wasn't offering us anything that we weren't doing already.

Later, I gave it some thought. I thought perhaps I wasn't being fair, thinking that when we would all grow up and get married, Mama would be left alone. I figured if we got married and Leo treated my mother well, then we wouldn't have to worry so much about Mama being left alone.

I guess I must have agreed because on December 14, 1934, they went and got married. We moved out of the neighborhood to half a block away from where his mother, stepchildren, and widowed sister were all living together. His other sister lived across the street. There weren't many houses around.

The first week they were wed, Mama went food shopping. When Papa, as we had to call him, came home from work, he asked her how much she'd spent. When she told him, he swung at her and hit her face. Mama was shocked and hurt. She put her hands to her chest, grabbed her housedress, and ripped it open saying to him, "Go ahead and kill me. I'm not used to walking a mile just for a pound of spaghetti. I shopped for a week when I only lived across the street from the grocery store." Our new home in the suburbs was at least three-fourths of a mile from any store.

Before Mama married Papa, she worked in the City; and we were doing all right. She used to tell us that if there was anything we needed while she was at work, that we could go to any store on the block and get what we needed. All we had to do was tell the store owner that Mama would pay for it when she came home from work. When she came home from work, we would tell her what we had bought; she'd give us the money, and we'd run across the street and pay for it. Mama had the storekeepers' respect and trust. Her boss where she worked and her fellow workers were fond of Mama, too.

Shortly after Mama was married, one Saturday morning after Papa had left for work, Maria, Vincenzina, and I went to lay down on the bed with Mama. Mama asked Maria to get her a glass of water. Rose was still in bed sleeping in our room. Rose had sharp hearing, she heard Mama ask Maria for a glass of water. Rose got up from bed and hid in the darkened doorway where Maria couldn't see her. Trying to be brave, Maria was going through the darkly lit dining room, without turning on the light. As she was about to pass our bedroom door to go into the kitchen, Rose stuck her hand out like a claw. Maria, afraid of her own shadow, screamed and froze. She pulled herself from chair to chair in slow motion trying to run. Mama, Vincenzina, and I jumped from the bed to see what had happened. Mama kept asking her, "What happened? What happened?" but Maria couldn't talk. She pointed towards our bedroom and with her hands imitated what Rose did. Mama went into the bedroom and Rose was pretending she was sound asleep. Maria kept pointing at Rose. Mama grabbed Rose by her hair, but Rose professed that she hadn't done anything. Rose was a jokester. As much as she protected Maria from anyone who would harm her, she took pleasure in scaring her at home at any opportunity she could.

One day, Papa made a one-sided egg sandwich. I began to make the same kind of sandwiches for my sisters and me for school lunches. I would beat up a couple of eggs, put oil in the frying pan, cut the Italian bread in the size of a wedge, then cut it in half and dip the cut side into the beaten eggs and fry only the dipped side of the bread. It really wasn't bad; it would be like an open fried egg sandwich.

Jean Milone

While Mama was working in the City sewing dresses, Papa would be working, too; sometimes it was busy at his place of work and sometimes it wasn't. When we came home from school, we would put the radio on to listen to *Just Plain Bill*. After the program was over, we'd turn the radio off and start our school homework. One day, Papa came home early and saw us still doing our homework. He yelled and asked, "Did you have the radio on?" He would go over to the Philco radio and touch it to see if it was still warm to see if we were lying about listening to it. I told him we did have it on for a little while but turned it off after the program finished to do our homework. He said he didn't want that radio on at all but to do our homework. He questioned everything all the time. We became very fearful of him.

Our kitchen was very small; it had a sink, stove, kitchen cabinets, and an icebox, but wasn't large enough for a kitchen table. The table was in a glassed-in porch. One summer evening while at the table, after we had finished dinner, my sisters and I were playing a guessing game trying to determine what object in the room someone was thinking of. Papa came into the porch and angrily asked, "Didn't you clean up yet?" And without a moment's notice, he picked up the four ends of the tablecloth and threw everything on the table—the glasses, dishes, utensils, etc.—right out the open window. His frequent erratic behavior frightened us to death. It seemed that no matter what we did, it upset him.

No wonder his mother wouldn't allow his stepdaughters to live with us. My mother was very disappointed that they weren't living with us since we kids all got along very well.

Papa was a WPA worker. He didn't work everyday; and if the weather wasn't so good, he was sent home. On this one day, he was home from work and did some cooking. When my sisters and I came home from school, he wasn't home. He had gone out. On the stove was a large covered pot with a wooden spoon through the pot's handles. I lifted up the cover to see what was in the pot. There were snails cooked in tomato sauce. I put the cover back on and slid the wooden spoon back through the handles. When he came home, he went directly to the pot and yelled, "Who touched this pot?" I said "No one, Pa." He shouted, "Don't lie to me. I left the wooden spoon facing down and now I find the wooden spoon facing up. So don't lie to me." I said, "Pa, I only looked to see what was in the pot. I didn't take any." He was furious and kept banging things around. I remembered then how before they were married, he had come to the house to convince me that we could listen to the radio, go to the movies, and do all the things that Mama already allowed us to do. Those privileges were gone.

Papa's sister had a son. One day, when he was thirteen years old, while riding his bicycle, he was struck by a car and thrown ten feet in the air. When he landed, another car dragged him almost half a block before stopping. The boy died. The whole family was devastated. Long after the funeral, Mama would go over to visit Papa's sister to see if she could do anything for her and to help to cheer her up. Once, while sitting at the table and talking with her sister-in-law, Mama noticed a bowl with walnuts on the table and that a walnut had three creases circled all around the nutshell instead of one. Mama picked it up and said, "Oh, look at this nut, it has three seams! This is supposed to be a good-luck walnut. Here, save it!"

The woman looked at her strangely. Unfortunately, she felt that Mama was into witchcraft. Mama was only trying to help her in her sadness. Mama never knew that his whole family didn't like her no matter how good she was to all of them.

Papa was involved in a club. I'm not sure whether it was Republican or Democratic. One of the members of the club lived on the next block from us. The member's son was having a fight with Papa's nephew. Papa sided with the member's son and argued with his own nephew and slapped him. Papa's family was outside and saw what was going on. They went to pull the nephew out and started beating on Papa. Mama was outside with the family; and when she saw them beating on her husband, she went to pull them off of him. Instead, they all turned on her. I went to pull Mama out, and they turned on me. They picked me up and threw me head first into a deep lot behind them filled with junk such as mattresses, refrigerators, bed springs, and so forth. When they pulled me out from the dump, I was soaking wet. I had urinated on myself and injured my back.

After this incident, Papa was on the outs with his family; and he decided to move. We moved further away into a rural area. There was not a house in sight. We had a beautiful and adorable black-haired puppy. It looked like a black-fur ball. My mother paid quite a bit of money for it. I was about to take the puppy for a walk so that he could do his business when Pa said "No! No! Let the dog out." He insisted that the dog would come back on his own when he was done. He wanted to train him, but he was a tiny puppy. Sadly, he never came back. We were all heartbroken. Rose was crying walking the streets looking for him. We assumed that someone seeing a tiny dog outdoors alone must have taken him.

Mama put a reward out for the puppy if he was found. Well, people brought us eleven dogs in all, none of which was ours. Mama managed to find each one of them a good family. The last dog was given to a family who had some farmland. They were very happy to have the dog. After a few days, we found the dog tied to a fence in our back yard yipping and wagging his tail. He had a nice collar and a good leather strap. It turned out that he didn't like to be alone; and if you didn't leave the light on for him, he would howl all night. We had to find him another home.

Mama did not like living in a rural neighborhood. She noticed that back in our old neighborhood there was a house that had been foreclosed. The house was on 101st Avenue across the street from Public School 64, the elementary school that we attended before Mama and Papa married. Mama went to the realtor, and they agreed to open the house. She agreed to take the bottom floor, pay rent, and take care of the furnace. We'd heat the house for us and for the top-floor tenant. So we moved.

It was in this house where so much happened. Papa wanted to adopt Vincenzina, and I forbid my mother to agree to it.

She was mine, and nobody was going to adopt her. He was so furious at me and said, "One of these days, I'm going to make you pee blood."

One night, we were having dinner and Papa had a piece of steak in his dish. By then we had gotten another dog. Papa cut the steak and gave Mama a piece. The dog went up to him, and he cut a piece of his steak and said "I'll give it to you, not to them." Is that how much he loved my little sister, whom he wanted to adopt? To avoid any argument, Mama cut her steak into small pieces; and while Papa was talking to the dog, she put the pieces of steak into a dish towel that she had on her lap, handed it to Vincenzina (who needed the nourishment the most), and told her to go into the kitchen to clean up. Thank God he didn't notice it.

Our kitchen was in the basement. It had an enclosed toilet, and next to it was the kitchen sink. On one end of the large kitchen, there was a wine cellar; and on the other side of the kitchen, there was the furnace room. Next to the furnace room there was the back door entrance. Vincenzina went to eat the pieces of meat in the furnace room.

Aunt Eleanor and Uncle Dom sent for their nephews, Frank and Paul, who had returned to Italy. Since her husband had died, Aunt Agatha wanted her two sons to return to America so that they could work and send her money. When they came, they got a furnished room, but they couldn't cook there. Paul was a barber, and his older brother Frank, who wasn't as good looking, had a beautiful singing voice. He also liked school and went to high school. Although they were first cousins, Paul fell in love with Margie. One day, Uncle Dom came to speak to Papa saying that Frank wanted to ask for my hand in marriage. My stepfather was delighted. He said, "Sure, I'll get some peanuts and frankfurters; and we'll celebrate." I said no. Papa was disappointed; so was Frank.

I felt terrible. I loved all my cousins, but I certainly didn't want to marry any of them. Boy! Would Papa have been happy if I got married and left home. He couldn't stand me.

Jean Milone

When I saw Uncle Dom, I approached him. I said "Zio, (Italian for *uncle*), what made you come for my hand in marriage to my cousin?" He felt bad knowing I was not interested in Frank as a husband. He said, "I had to. He asked me to represent him, and you don't refuse. It's your duty when you're asked. That's all I did." He was sorry.

Papa was such a suspicious man. Once, my sisters and I went to the movies. It was getting dark when we got out. We were all holding hands as we came upon a wonderful bakery shop with gorgeous cakes. We pressed our noses against the window wishing, "Someday I'll buy that cake with all that whipped cream and strawberries on it" many times. Or one of us would say, "I'd like that chocolate cake." On this one occasion we strolled by each store along the way imagining what it would be like to get whatever we wanted when we got older.

As we were looking from one store window to another, I noticed someone dodging from one store doorway to another, until we got home. I got nervous and then realized it was Papa following us to see what we were doing.

Later, he questioned us about what we did after the movie. He wanted to trap us in any way he could because he told us that he was following us and wanted to see if we would lie about it. He was very distrusting.

It was also embarrassing to me when I had to ask him for twenty-five cents to buy a pair of mercerized silk-like stockings. While I stood there waiting, he would dig his hand into his pocket for the longest time until he pulled out a quarter.

We were not extravagant and never bought anything unnecessary because we knew how hard Mama struggled. When she said we couldn't go to the movies, we didn't question it; we understood. It killed me to see her cry.

She always had the icebox filled with all that was absolutely necessary. Even in the apartment she had before she got married where we didn't have a large icebox. In that apartment, the kitchen had twin tubs with the covers on them to wash clothes. In one tub she bathed us; in the other tub, she had a cake of ice that the iceman would deliver and used it as an icebox.

In winter, when Papa came home from work, he'd ask Mama to pull his pants off. Rose would do it so that Mama didn't have to. He wore long johns. He would always say how lucky we were that he was better than our own father because he always worked in all kinds of weather. He used to want Mama to bathe his feet. Instead, Rose would volunteer so Mama wouldn't have to do that either.

No wonder his stepchildren from his second wife were petrified of him. His own mother knew Papa's temperament and she wouldn't let him have those children after he married my mother either. Instead, they lived with her and his widowed sister after their mother died. They were nice kids, and we got along very well with them. We felt bad when the girls would get mail from their mother's relatives in Italy. He had to read the letters to them, and always managed to make them cry. We felt so bad for them. They would always make the sign of the cross before entering our apartment.

One day, there was a circus parade coming to our area, and Rose asked Mama if she could go and watch the parade. Mama told her to make sure she came right home after the parade had gone by. Rose took Vincenzina with her. They walked along with the parade and saw all the clowns, the animals in their cages, and the musicians that were part of the circus. When the girls didn't return home, we went out looking for them. We finally found them watching the workers scurrying around as they were putting up the tents and doing their jobs. Mama scolded both of them. It was a good thing that Papa wasn't home yet.

When I graduated elementary school, I won first prize in sewing class. I won a medal every year, but this time I got a five-dollar prize. When I came home, I gave it to Mama. There was no celebration nor did I expect any. We had a lemon salad, which was good because it was made with very large lemons, but I didn't complain.

Jean Milone

I went to John Adams High School. I loved it. I wanted an education so much, but I had to quit because I had to go to work. I attended night school until I turned sixteen, but I never finished, or received my GED because Papa did everything he could to make it difficult for me. I would take a ten o'clock bus to return home by ten thirty. If I missed that bus, the next bus wouldn't get me home until eleven; and I'd come home to find that he had locked the door. Mama would unlock the door. He'd be in bed and Mama used to want me to call out to let him know that I was home. I used to feel so hurt by his mistrusting me that I'd refuse to call out. I knew she would get heartaches because of me. I'd be upset because if I was up to no good, I could have stepped out of my window onto the garbage pail and go wherever I wanted to go, but I was not of that kind.

I went to work and when I got paid, I'd give Mama my pay envelope. Mama wanted me to give it to Papa. I refused. I told her that I'd give it to her; and if she wanted to hand it over to him, she could do it. Then it aggravated me that when I needed stockings, I had to go to him and stand like a beggar for the twenty-five cents it cost to buy them.

Papa didn't allow my cousins from Italy to come to the house not even to see Mama. He didn't want anyone to come to our place. Next door to us was a gas station, and the owner knew how difficult our circumstances were with my stepfather.

In the back of the house there was a small plot where Mama planted vegetables. Mama would ask us to go out in front of the house and sweep up the horse manure to put it into her vegetable garden. With a pan and brush we did it and put it in the garden. God bless her; she planted so many things in that small area, and everything grew beautifully. She had a green thumb for gardening, and the vegetables helped to feed her nephews, Aunt Agatha's sons Frank and Paul. Mama used to cook the vegetables, and put the food in containers. Then, with the gas station owner's approval, she would place the containers between the gas stand sign, and he would watch to make sure that no one other than one of my cousins would pick them up.

Under a Black Star

Once, Mama was in a bus, and the bus had an accident. It hit into a pole, and Mama injured her leg. She bled badly. She didn't sue, but was given eighty dollars as a settlement. She gave Papa the money, and he bought crates of grapes to make wine. We all helped him, including Mama, squeeze the grapes. Mama tried to please him in every way she could. He did make good wine.

In the kitchen, we had our big dining room table with six large, heavy-legged chairs. On occasion, a member of Papa's club would come to the house to bring him some material pertaining to the club. He was a tall, good-looking man with a mustache. In fact, he was handsome. When Papa noticed that he was giving me some attention, he made sure not to have him bring anything to the house any more.

Every night, Mama and I took care of the furnace. We'd shake the ashes out and shovel fresh coals over the hot coals, and watch it till the coals got a good start to heat up, and then we would bank it for the night. Papa never had anything to do with it and didn't know how. Once, Papa, who regularly came home drunk, entered the furnace room and started shaking the furnace and letting all the hot coals out. Mama ran in to stop him, but he already had all the red hot coals shaken out. Mama said, "We took care of it for the night!" and tried to stop him. She told him to go to bed. She bent down to separate the ashes from the red-hot coals to start the fire again. He grabbed her by the neck as she was bent over and tried to put her face into the red-hot coals. We all screamed. I grabbed him by the wrist to stop him while I was screaming "No, Pa, don't do that!" He got so angry. He grabbed me and threw me into the coal bin. If the coal bin had been full, I wouldn't have gone so far down. The bin was almost empty, but I got hold of his tie and hung on to it. With my legs, I was able to hold on to the edge of the bin and not go down all the way into the bottom of the bin. Mama pushed him out of the furnace room and told him to go to bed, which he did. He was so drunk. Needless to say, we had to start the furnace all over again. It took time, and we ended up going to bed very late into the morning.

Jean Milone

My sisters and I all slept in one bedroom. Maria, Rose, and Vincenzina slept in one bed; and I slept on a folding cot right against the wall near the door. I would sit up at the edge of the cot with my ear to the door waiting for Papa to come home—usually late and drunk—to see if he was going to get violent with Mama, as he had done so often before. Once, she was sitting up waiting for him in the living room. He came in drunk, and when she simply asked him if he had locked the door, he got so angry that he punched her in her breast. Mama never said a word just not to start anything or wake us children up. Little did he know that I was awake and knew everything that was happening. Oh, what a foolish man he was! Had he been good to my mother, it would have made my sisters and me very happy. He also would have been well respected by Mama's family. Instead, he took advantage of the fact that he knew that Mama's family was against her marriage to him and that they wouldn't come to visit.

He even had the nerve to go to the factory where Mama and Maria worked. Mama no longer worked in the City; the factory was near home. He climbed a flight of steps and went to talk to the boss to ask him how much Mama's and Maria's salaries were. The boss felt he was a disturbed man and told him that if he didn't leave, he would throw him down the flight of stairs. The incident embarrassed Mama; now her coworkers were aware of Mama's circumstances.

In the morning, Papa would have six eggs and half a bottle of wine. He knew that Mama wouldn't go to her sister or brother and tell them the problems or trouble she was having with him, and he knew that they wouldn't interfere. Mama was trying to make the marriage work because she was ashamed that the family was against her marriage.

My poor mother had such high hopes for a better life by marrying Papa. Mama, to make money, even made shorts for children so that Maria and I could go from door to door selling them for twenty-five cents, and fifty cents for a more detailed pair. She sure was misled by this midwife who declared that Papa was a wonderful, loving, endearing, hardworking man.

Under a Black Star

The midwife knew Mama loved children, and she dwelled on her sympathy for them. As I said earlier, it was long after they were married that we learned how the midwife came to know my stepfather.

One day, while Papa wasn't home, Aunt Eleanor and my cousins surprised us and came to see us. Aunt Eleanor and the rest of the family couldn't stand him. Aunt Eleanor realized how bad things were for Mama, and she encouraged my mother to leave him. Mama felt bad because she wanted so much to be with her family; yet, she wanted her marriage to work. She had hoped he would be more cautious knowing that her family was close by, but that never happened.

Mama had a friend who survived an earthquake in Italy. She and her brother were buried by the earthquake and found alive a couple of days later. They had had only two lemons between them to eat. One day, after coming to America, she came to visit us. Papa was at the club. We didn't have anything to serve her, so she said she'd be right back and left the house. She was back within fifteen minutes with a cake for us kids and some buns.

In the meantime, Papa came home and told her it was late and to leave the house and go home. She was insulted. She said to him, "I came to help." He told her he didn't need her help. She replied, "I didn't come for you. I came for your family." My mother was beginning to lose her spunk. She assured her friend not to pay attention to him because he wasn't feeling too well. She stayed for about an hour and then left.

As was the Italian custom, when company would come to visit, we would put the coffee on and put out cookies, liquor, or wine. On this particular occasion, a couple who were friends of Mama's came to visit. We put on the coffee pot, set the table with cups, spoons, napkins, sugar, and Ritz crackers, which were the newest crackers out. I put out a Pyrex bowl filled with Ritz crackers on the table. Mama had asked Papa to get a pitcher of wine. This was the wine that was made with the money Mama gave him from her bus accident. He refused. So Mama took the pitcher and headed toward the wine cellar to get the wine. He became furious when he saw her defy him. He picked up the dining room chair, and while Mama had her back turned, he raised the chair with the intention to hit her on the head with it. I saw that and I screamed "Pa, don't!" At the same time, I picked up the bowl with the Ritz crackers and swung it at him; and it hit his hand. Well, he became enraged. He put down the chair and as quick as lightning, grabbed a hot cup of coffee and smashed it into my face. The force of his hand broke my rimless eye-glasses and my nose. A piece of the lens pierced a blood vessel and stuck into a bone in my nose. The blood streamed all over my face and clothes.

The couple screamed and Mama turned. She didn't know he had attempted to strike her with the chair. She was stunned when she saw blood shooting from my nose and down my face. Mama went wild. As small as she was, she amazingly got the strength to grab him by his hair, drag him to the back door, and throw him out. Then she came to me. I was in shock and hadn't moved. Mama gently pulled the glass out of the bone of my nose. Once the glass was out, she was able to take care of the bleeding. I'm sure he went to the club to sleep. It all happened so fast that the company couldn't help. They felt terrible and were very shaken up by the incident. After everything quieted down, they left.

The next night, he was back in the house. I couldn't bare it anymore. I knew it would never change. I decided to leave. I told my sisters where I was going. I packed a few belongings; but before I left, with my savings in change, I stopped to see Mr. Gene at the grocery store to pay our bill that was in trust for nineteen dollars. Mr. Gene had tears in his eyes. He had known us since we were little kids. He never asked nor said anything about the bandaged nose. I just said, "I came to pay our bill." I paid, said good-bye, and left. He knew that our lives had become very difficult.

I took the bus to Jamaica Avenue and transferred at the terminal to get a bus going to Astoria. I was going to Zia Peppina's house. I was not a mean person; I was and I am a very affectionate and kind person. I knew how Mama had suffered all her life and I didn't want to hurt her. She was so good to everyone, had sympathy for everyone, and tried to help everyone. I only left because she took Papa back, and I couldn't handle the abuse any more. Mama had lost her spunk. I left with the same bloody clothes I had on the night before. Papa never apologized for anything he did wrong.

I wouldn't go to Aunt Eleanor's or Uncle Dom's because I knew there would be a lot of trouble involved since they were dead set against Mama marrying Papa. Zia Peppina and Marianna had a two-room apartment, a bedroom, a kitchen, and a bathroom, of course. When Zia Peppina saw me, she was shocked to see how I looked. "Of course," she said "you can stay with us." Zia and Marianna slept at the head of the bed and I slept at their feet. Zia didn't want rent from me, but I'd put the money inside the back of a picture frame—something Marianna knew about.

I continued working as a seamstress at Treo, which manufactured girdles and brassieres, in Jamaica, New York. I was making fifteen dollars a week. At times I was a model for one of their designers. After a week, Mama came to see me at work. She asked me to come back home. I knew she loved me and needed me. I felt terrible to say, "No, not while he's there." I would go see Mama and my sisters from time to time when he wasn't home, and they would beg me to stay.

During one visit, I saw what looked like a bottle covered with a dinner cloth on the kitchen table. I was about to pick up the cloth when Maria said, "Don't touch." She showed me that at the end of each corner of the dinner cloth was a number to see if any one would disturb it. It was covering a bottle of wine. How could I go back home? He hadn't changed at all.

It was a few months later that Mama had finally had enough. She wanted all her children with her, and my sisters were constantly asking for me. Mama moved out without telling Papa. She rented a first-floor railroad apartment on Gates Avenue, in Brooklyn. Across the street from the apartment was a synagogue. On the same block, there was a dress factory and a grocery store. I don't know how she did it, and all by herself.

Her old spunk was back. Of course, I went back to living with Mama; we were all so very happy.

A few months later, Papa located my mother and made arrangements to meet and talk to her. They met at an outdoor location. He wanted Mama to come back. She told him she couldn't afford to move again because she didn't have the money. He said to her, "You and your daughter work; you should have enough to move." Mama said, "Forget it" and had a legal separation.

She began working in the dress shop a few doors away from our Brooklyn apartment. Everyone loved Mama. She was always on the jolly side. I was the worrywart. I cared for Mama like she was my child. Mama always said, "If your door steps don't smile, no one will come to visit you. Everyone has their own problems; they don't want to come visit you to hear your problems." Mama was a new woman; she was her old self.

I joined the choir at St. Barbara's Church. St. Barbara's Church was beautiful. It had a wonderful choir of about fifty members. We had a terrific music teacher. He was simply fantastic. All the choir members had operatic-like voices. I had a good voice, and they were glad to have me. All the railroad apartment buildings were attached. Looking out the windows in the back of the building, you could see clotheslines running across all the back yards. I was always singing in my soprano voice. I wanted so much to be a singer. It was so easy for me to sing. I could not understand why people couldn't sing or didn't have the voice to sing. It was really nice because whenever I'd finish singing, I'd hear applauses from the people hanging out their clothes, or they would be out their window to listen. We were all so happy there.

A few months later, Zia Peppina and Marianna came to visit us, and Marianna took me out to the movies. When we came back from the movies, I opened the door and everyone yelled, "Surprise!" It was my eighteenth birthday. Wow! What a different life I was living!

Dad. Circa 1920.

Maria and me before Rose was born. 1925.

Newspaper clipping: Mama pregnant with Vincenzina;
with me, Rose, and Maria. June 21, 1929.

Vincenzo Nanfro. (Mama's second husband
and Vincenza's father.) 1929.

Mama and Leonardo Ventura.
(Mama's third husband.) 1934.

Zia Peppina. 1943.

Mama at Joseph's Dress Factory. Circa 1935.

Under a Black Star

Me, Maria, Vincenzina, and Rose. I cut my stepfather
"Papa" out of the photograph. Circa 1936.

One Sunday morning before going to church, I asked
Maria and Rose to clean some chicken feathers that weren't
removed too well at the chicken market. I told them that when
I got home I would prepare the meal. Mama had gone to visit
a sick friend to help her. After about an hour, I came home
from church to find both my sisters plucking the hairs out of
the chicken with a pair of tweezers. The chickens didn't come
clean and wrapped in packages like they do in the supermarkets
today. With the very fine hairs on the chicken, we'd take the
chicken over the gas flame from the stove and singe the hairs.
That was the last time I'd ask them to clean a chicken!

Mama would take us to the movies and pay adult prices
for us when they gave away dishes. She wanted to make a
set for each one of us. She insisted on holding the dishes for
fear we'd drop them. Mama loved cowboy and Indian movies.
In one movie scene with Errol Flynn, he was crouched down
to shoot one of the Indians when above the rocks was an

Indian who was about to jump Errol. Mama got excited. She wanted to warn Errol and yelled, "Look out!" Errol turned and as the Indian jumped, Errol shot him. Mama forgot she had the platters on her lap. She raised her arms to clap and the dishes slipped off her lap and crashed on the floor into many pieces. Of course, the entire audience in the theater roared with laughter. She did eventually manage to get a set of dishes for each of us, although we did have some pieces missing.

While living in Brooklyn, we were finally enjoying life with peace, love, and joy. My sisters were very attractive young girls. There was a very handsome-looking fellow that wanted so much to go out with Maria. He had a missing thumb. When he was five or six years old, a merry-go-round truck would come every week and the children would run out and pay to get on. He had caught his thumb on the merry-go-round wheel that turns the riding horse. Maria did like him but she was terribly shy and the young fellow knew it. He was persistent in asking her out, and she finally agreed to go out with him. When they walked outdoors together, Maria would look at the store windows and didn't make any conversation. Not a word. Finally, he said to her, "Maria, do you like chicken?" She answered, "Yes." And he responded, "Well, then take a wing!" meaning take his arm, which she did. Unfortunately, when she learned that he was studying to become an undertaker, and she was deadly frightened about that, she quickly ended that courtship. It was a shame. He was a very nice guy.

There was a house for sale on Eighty-Fourth Street in Ozone Park next to my Uncle Dom's neighbor that we wanted to buy. All the houses were semiattached homes. We were all excited about the idea of returning to our old neighborhood and living on the same street as Aunt Eleanor and Uncle Dom. So the time came, fifteen years later, when Mama asked Uncle Frank for the deposit that she had put on her old house that he and Aunt Eleanor and family were living in. He refused. He felt she had lost the house and he shouldn't have to give her anything. He forgot what he had promised Mama. Although it was true that if they didn't take it over, it would have been lost, they never had to put a deposit down, they just assumed the payments and had a house to live in. It would have taken them years to afford a deposit to buy a house of their own. Later, Aunt Eleanor came with her son, Frankie, one night and gave Mama the money they owed her. We knew she had had to fight with Uncle Frank to get the money.

Mama was so happy. She had always wanted a home of her own. Aunt Eleanor and Uncle Dom were happy, too, that Mama was now able to live close to them in her own home. We all loved each other so much. We would always hug and kiss each other.

Uncle Dom got a heart attack. He didn't believe he could get a heart attack because one day he ran to catch a bus and he happily told us, "See. If I had heart trouble, I would have died while running!" I got so angry at him and told him, "What would you have proved if you had dropped dead? You have got to stay alive because you have to take us four girls down the aisle when we get married." He was thrilled to learn that we wanted him to walk us down the aisle. He did live long enough to walk us all down the aisle. We loved him dearly.

Most of the homes on the block were converted from single to two-family homes. We had a completely finished kitchen in the basement, which was very nice. Upstairs, on the first floor there were a living room and two bedrooms and a front porch. The second floor was rented to a lovely couple with a child.

One night, Maria got into bed before Rose had come upstairs. So, she got the idea, since Rose would have to stand in bed and reach up to pull the light chain, that when she sat back down, Maria would stick out her thumb so Rose would be goosed. Maria felt that this was her opportunity to get back at Rose for all the times Rose played pranks on her. Instead, Rose flopped back on the bed and almost broke Maria's thumb. This time, Rose got into trouble without doing anything. Maria had to wear a splint on her thumb. Mama didn't say anything. She realized that it was Maria's fault this time and not Rose's. Mama knew that Maria wanted to get back at Rose for all the teasing Rose had done to her over the years.

Jean Milone

Our dog, Beauty, was a great dog. She was always with Mama. Even when she went to bed, Beauty would sleep next to Mama's side of the bed. When Mama went out, Beauty would be behind her. This day, Mama was going to the corner grocery store when a car came careening down the street and would have hit Mama, but Beauty nipped Mama on her leg and Mama jumped up on the sidewalk. Beauty was hit, instead, and the car never stopped. Thankfully, she recovered from her injuries.

One weekend during the summer of 1944, we went with Aunt Eleanor's family to their summer home in Lake Carmel. It was very nice. We could walk down the hill and go swimming in the lake. There was no bathroom in the house. We had to go out to the outhouse. One night, when we all went to the outhouse, Uncle Frank decided to have some fun. He put a white sheet over his head and body and began w-oo-ing like a ghost towards the outhouse. Maria, who was afraid of her own shadow, saw the white figure and got so frightened that she sprinted back toward the house screaming. She blasted into the room (it's a wonder she didn't go through the screen door) and collapsed. Mama and Aunt Eleanor were frightened and didn't know what had happened. When they finally found out, Aunt Eleanor got very angry at Uncle Frank. He laughed thinking it was very funny. He didn't realize that Maria would react the way she did. He was sorry.

While there, Mama wasn't feeling too well. In fact, she was lying down on the couch most of the time. When we got home the next day, we were still unpacking boxes from moving. Margie was helping us. After a while, Mama suddenly passed out onto the kitchen floor. She threw up; and while coming to, she was trying to pick up the vomit into her cupped hands. We picked her up and put her on a chair and cleaned her up. She wanted to get up from the chair because in her mind she thought she had had a stroke. We allowed her to stand with help and she was relieved that it wasn't a stroke. But she did have pain under her arm. When I went to look under her arm, she had a lump the size of an egg. That lump slipped out when she tried to hold onto the chair, and she passed out again with her arm extended.

~

We went to our family doctor, in Brooklyn, at the first available appointment. We had to travel by train for an hour. The doctor examined Mama and told her she had to go for a biopsy. When I took her to the hospital, the nurse took her upstairs to put her to bed. Then I would be able to see her. While waiting in the hallway, I saw Mama walking towards me. I asked her what had happened, and she told me that the nurse wanted to put her in bed with sheets that were used by a previous patient. She told them, "I don't mind if I stay in the sheets for a week, as long as they are clean when I first lie on them. It's my own body." I explained to the doctor. He was disturbed because all the doctors were ready for the surgery. I told the doctor that I didn't blame my mother and asked them to change the sheets. He explained to us that because of the war, they had a shortage of nurses and they couldn't wash or press the sheets too often; but they changed the sheets—they were wrinkled but clean.

After they took a biopsy, we went home. I was to call the doctor in a couple of days for the results. When I called the doctor, to my dismay, I heard what I never thought I'd hear—Mama had cancer. How was I going to tell Mama the real problem and get her back into the hospital? The doctor told me they would have to remove her breast. Cancer was a hush, hush word in the 1940s. I told Mama that they didn't take enough out for the biopsy. I felt so guilty for lying. I knew that if Mama had known that her breast was going to be removed, then she wouldn't have gone back to the hospital. When she awoke after the operation, she said to me, "You tricked me, you traitor." I felt awful. I did trick her. I only did it to save her life.

While she was in the hospital, she was in a ward with about ten patients. Mama was in a lot of pain. She was cut completely across from one breast to the other, then from her shoulder down to her stomach. It looked like a cross with all the stitches. At the time they did not do therapy like they do now.

I wanted to care for Mama around the clock when she was in the hospital, but because I had to go to work, I hired a private nurse. Mama kept saying, "She hurts me." I tried to explain to her that naturally it was going to hurt because she had had a big surgery. One day, I was there when the nurse came in with a bag. It looked like a big five-pound bag of sugar (sugar was sold in five-pound cheesecloth bags then). It may have been a bag of sand, but I really don't know. I watched the nurse pick up Mama's arm with no gentleness and shove the bag right into her armpit with such force. My mother whimpered and the nurse said, "Don't be such a baby." I fired her on the spot. I got Mama much better nurses, and she had a nurse around the clock.

Aunt Eleanor came to the house and gave me two hundred fifty dollars for Mama's nurses. I refused the money saying, "We'll pay for it." She got very angry at me and shouted, "She's my sister and I want to help." She was right, and I accepted it.

Mama was in the hospital a whole week until she was able to come home to her own bed. She really was a good patient. I took care of medicating and dressing her stitches. She was in a happy spirit and always ready to joke. After a while, we didn't want Mama to be alone upstairs. So, we decided to get Mama out of bed and bring her downstairs with us. Rose, would stand behind Mama and put her arms around her waist, then we'd put Mama's feet on top of Rose's feet and walk her to the steps. Naturally, we would guard against her falling. Mama was beginning to lose her eyesight. After the surgery, she got diabetes. We knew very little about cancer, or diabetes, at that time. The doctor said she may have gotten it as a result of the surgery. I had to give her diabetic shots. We did not know of any other family members who had had cancer or diabetes.

Gradually, Mama got weaker, but we continued to have her downstairs in the kitchen with us. She never complained, and sometimes we had her sitting in the back yard on a nice summer or fall day with one or two of us and always with Beauty by her side.

Under a Black Star

Mama's condition worsened and she became bedridden. Being such a worrywart, I was constantly thinking of Mama. One day, I was on the train coming home from the dress factory with our neighbor, Mrs. Mancino, who also worked there. In fact, she had gotten the job for me. While standing on the express train holding onto the hand strap, I passed out. I remember hearing my friend crying and saying to the people who picked me up, "Her mother is very sick." We were on the express train and couldn't get off until the next stop. Normally, we would connect with another train on the opposite side of the platform to get to our home station, and then walk several blocks to our home. Instead, my friend took me out on to the platform and told me to sit on the platform bench. She called her son, Danny, to come to pick us up. She was afraid for me to take the next train home. I was grateful Danny came. Mrs. Mancino was so considerate of me and cared for me as if I were her daughter. She was a dear friend to me.

Marie, Rose, and I always brought our pay envelope to Mama. Even though I ran the household, we'd bring my mother the pay. I didn't want Mama to feel she didn't count anymore. If I had not had my sisters' cooperation, I would not have been able to pay the house bills— food, phone, oil heating, hospital, train fares. We didn't have hospitalization insurance. We had to pay everything in cash. I would tell Maria and Rose to make sure that they counted the money in their pay envelopes before coming home to make sure there were no errors. Vincenzina was still going to high school. I used to stop after work at an Italian food store to get things that Mama would like to eat when she could. Eating was becoming more difficult for her. One day, she put a shriveled black Greek olive in her mouth. I don't know what made me buy them. I stuck my finger into her mouth and scooped the olive out thinking I was doing it for her own good. Had I known she was dying, I would not have deprived her from eating anything she wanted, but I thought I was prolonging her life.

We loved Mama so much. She struggled her whole life for us. I used to think, I don't care if she sits in a corner blind from diabetes, as long as she is alive. My friends told me that

I was being very selfish because she was the one suffering, not me. When they said that to me, I didn't understand them; and I disliked them. She was my mother, not theirs. It got to the point when we couldn't bring her downstairs anymore.

I would give my sisters an allowance for train fare, and they'd take lunch from home. My sisters knew things were tough and realized the reason I ran the house with a strong hand. At times, they may have resented this, but they never said a word. They did respect me and loved me. None of my sisters or my Aunt Eleanor knew of my mother's bad condition. They only knew that she was sick, but not that she was dying.

One day, Aunt Eleanor said that she wanted to go see Mama's doctor with me. If she had known how to get to him, she would have gone to see him by herself. We took the train and went to see the doctor. The doctor explained that the punch in the breast Mama had gotten from her husband had developed into cancer. When the doctor told Aunt Eleanor that Mama was going to die, I shrunk down in the chair. Mama had not wanted Aunt Eleanor to know how bad she was. Mama had said to me, "Gina, 'la mama,' don't tell my sister how sick I am, or she'll die like a little bird." Aunt Eleanor knew I was carrying the burden all by myself. Mama knew that she would never get well. She would say, "For me to be well again, I would have to be reborn." She also told me, "Don't worry. I'll try not to frighten any of you when I die." She meant she wouldn't scream or whine when in pain, and she didn't.

While bedridden at home, we couldn't afford a nurse. So, I went to the high school and spoke to the principal and explained our situation. I wanted to take Vincenzina out of school so that she could take care of Mama while Maria, Rose, and I went to work.

The principal said it was not possible because the law wouldn't allow it. She was underage. Vincenzina didn't know the severity of Mama's illness. I promised the principal that when Mama was gone, Vincenzina would be back in school because she loved school so much. If one of us who worked had to stay home, we couldn't make ends meet to pay all of our expenses. The principal felt compassionate and said she'd let Vincenzina stay home but that she had to return when Mama was gone.

It was also near Christmas time, and it would be Mama's last Christmas. I knew Mama wouldn't be with us for long; but I didn't tell my sisters, and I didn't have the heart to have a Christmas tree. I just told my sisters I didn't want a Christmas tree.

At that time, Rose was sick in bed with a fever. She insisted on getting a Christmas tree. I'm glad she did. I was wrong not to want one. I tried so hard not to let them know. It was a bitter cold winter night and snowing. My sisters pitched in whatever money they had to buy a tree. They had to go to the city line for a tree.

It was the last night to sell trees. The girls gave the man whatever money they had, and he gave them a tree. All three of them carried the tree home over a mile and a half in the bitter cold. The tree was a tall and beautiful tree, big and full. We had a very high ceiling; still we had to snip the top of the tree off so we could put the star on top. I'm so glad that my sisters got the tree and that Mama was able to see her last Christmas tree. It was beautifully decorated, thanks to my sisters.

At times, Mama would get lonely in bed so she'd bang as hard as she could with the bell we left on the side of the bed to call us in case she needed us. This time, she banged so hard that we were all tripping over one another running up the stairway to get to her fast. We didn't know what had happened. Upon entering the room, she smiled and said, "When I die, you'll be watching me for three days; watch me now while I'm still alive." So, we'd sit with her and joke around after that. She'd tell us many proverbs that all made sense. Of course, they were all told in Italian.

There was no TV then, and Mama said many times that some day we'd be having movies in the house. To think she was right—we have TV in our homes now!

Friends from the shop where Mama worked used to come to visit unannounced in groups of three or four people. They would report back to their coworkers, raving at how immaculately clean, fresh smelling, and well-kept Mama was.

There was never an odor of urine or any smell of sickness in the room. If she tipped the bedpan too much and it spilled over, we told her it was our fault and immediately changed her and the sheets. Mama was always washed and powdered, and she never got a bed sore.

Beauty would always be at Mama's bedside. Mama would reach down her hand, and the dog would get up from her lying position and make it easier for Mama to touch or pet her. That dog understood everything. If she could have talked, she probably would have.

Several months had gone by. Then one day when I came home from work, Vincenzina was upset and worried. She said to me, "Jean, Mama won't wake up and won't eat." I immediately called the doctor that lived in our vicinity, and he came as fast as he could. He told me Mama was in a coma. He was going to call the ambulance, but I told him not to. If she was going to die, she might as well die at home. The doctor said to me "Jean, if your mother has a chance to survive, you're going to feel terrible that you deprived her of that chance." I felt he was right and agreed. But he knew she would never come home. He didn't want her to die at home for us to see. The doctor said Mama would never have lived for a year and a half after her surgery had she been cared for in the hospital instead of at home with such love and care. Before going into a coma, Mama had been complaining of severe headaches. The cancer had metastasized to her brain. The doctor had advised us to get a specialist to come and see Mama. The specialist came and advised to have the top of her head cut open like a trap door to relieve the pressure. I declined. I knew Mama wouldn't want that, since she knew she was going to die. Why mess up her body any further.

Seemingly like mental telepathy, it's strange that although only the doctor was called, Aunt Eleanor and Mrs. Mancino came to the house at the same time. They tried to comfort us when the ambulance picked Mama up to take her out. One day before Mama went into a coma, while my sisters and I were on the train on our way to work, we met the wife of a cousin of Mama's. Very bluntly and without any finesse she asked, "Did you get your mother's dress for the funeral yet?" I was shocked that she would ask such a question in front of my sisters. I had never told them how seriously ill Mama was. If they knew, they never said a word to me, but I think they understood.

While Mama was in a coma at the hospital, I did make a call to the undertaker to find out about my father's grave. I asked if there was room for another burial. He told me there was, and I let it go at that. I went to see Mama every day right from work. I used to sing her favorite songs to her and talk. I knew she heard me, but didn't say anything. Once, with her eyes closed she said to me, "Did you call the undertaker?" My hair on my arms stood up on ends. How did she know? While she was in the hospital, within a week of her stay there, her back became full with black bedsores; and she used to be left wet. No catheter was used. I began to stay with her in the hospital from morning till night. I would sing songs that she liked. Sometimes, she seemed to come out of the coma for a second and say to me, "If I ever go home, I'd like to take the one that sings to me home." She never knew it was me singing to her. She'd fall right back into the coma. Mama was getting worse. Once, with closed eyes, she said "There are two angels calling me, they're my twin babies." I kept watching Mama. A woman who was sitting up in her bed near us with her arms wrapped around her waist rocking back and forth with pain called out to me saying, "Don't keep watching her, otherwise she won't be able to die. Let her be." That afternoon, Aunt Eleanor and my sisters came after work. They didn't want me to stand there and watch Mama die. At one point, Mama's whole body jumped up like she got an electric shock and her whole body went down just as fast. She died later that same day on September 19, 1946. I guess she waited till we were all together. She was fifty years old.

~

Jean Milone

When we came home from the hospital, we sat in our kitchen with not a word between us. It seemed as if we were all in shock. Aunt Eleanor was there, too. We tried to make conversation, but didn't know what to say. Then Uncle Frank came down and asked Aunt Eleanor to come home. She told him she was staying for a while. He insisted that she leave with him telling her, "You can't do anything here, so what are you doing here." She couldn't take it anymore and screamed "I'll go when I'm ready. She was my sister, and I want to be here for a while. So go home."

The wake was held at home. Funeral parlors were uncommon back then. Our living room furniture was emptied out into another room. Mama was to be laid out for three days. The house was filled with flowers from the floor up to the ceiling and filled with people, too.

Beauty kept trying to come in from the downstairs kitchen. We wouldn't let her in, and she would stay behind the door. Every time anyone came through that back door, she'd try to sneak in. The visitors came from the front door and the back door.

On the last evening after everyone was gone, we all agreed to see what the dog would do. So, we put a chair close to the coffin and we opened the door to let Beauty in. She went directly to the living room, got on the chair, and leaned over the coffin. She whimpered, sniffed Mama's face and hands, and then got off the chair. With her tail between her legs, she went straight downstairs to the kitchen with never a sound.

On the day of the funeral, the undertaker picked up the flowers in the room to take to the cemetery. People arrived at our house to say their last good-byes to Mama. When it was time for our farewell, I didn't expect Maria to go up to Mama to say good-bye. Instead, I saw her bend down and kiss Mama. That shocked me, and I passed out for the longest time. The doctor was called, and most of the people were making all kinds of suggestions as to how to bring me to. Uncle Frank was getting impatient and wanted to have the casket closed. He wanted to leave me home, and continue with the funeral. It's a good thing the doctor, Uncle Dom, Aunt

Eleanor, and my sisters said no. They waited till I came to, and took me to the casket to kiss Mama good-bye.

Later, after the funeral, I found out what Uncle Frank had wanted to do. Luckily they didn't listen to Uncle Frank. I would have had her casket dug up and opened so that I could have the opportunity to say my last good-byes. I wouldn't have cared how much it cost.

~

When we finally went back to work, Vincenzina stayed home. She hadn't been feeling too well after Mama died. If she was downstairs in the kitchen and had to go upstairs to fix the beds, she would be afraid to go up by herself. So, she'd call Beauty to go with her, but the dog wouldn't go. She had to take her by the collar and drag her upstairs and close the door shut so that she wouldn't run down without her. After Mama was gone, the dog would not go upstairs at all.

Eventually, Vincenzina went back to high school. She wanted to graduate with her class, but she had missed two and a half terms—they had two terms within a year. The principal felt that she wouldn't be able to catch up with her class and said that she would have to get a doctor's note stating that she was able to handle the stress of studying for all of her tests. Vincenzina insisted that she could do it. My sister was bright to begin with. Even as a child, she would memorize a whole book word for word. The principal did get a letter from the doctor. Vincenzina passed all her tests and was able to graduate with her class. She also got a scholarship to Oswego College. Unfortunately, I didn't allow her to go to college even with her scholarship. We were good girls, but people assumed that without Mama we would be free as birds and go wild. Imagine what people would have said if I had let her go to college! Besides, not many girls went to college back then, only fellows. Some of the neighbors were so busy watching what we did that they neglected to notice what their own children were up to.

Mama on Gates Avenue after she left Papa. 1940.

Rose, me, Maria, Mama, and
Vincenzina on Gates Avenue. 1940.

Mama, Uncle Domenic, and Aunt Eleanor. 1940.

Maria, me, Rose, Mama, and Vincenzina. 1943.

Vincenzina, Cousin Margie, Maria, me,
and Rose, in Lake Carmel. 1944.

Mama sick at Lake Carmel. We didn't know at
that time that she had cancer. 1944.

Maria, Vincenzina, Mama, and me, in our backyard on 84th Street, Ozone Park. June 1946.

Mama in our kitchen on 84th Street, just before returning to the hospital before she died. 1946.

Beauty, our dog.

Maria, me, and Vincenzina, at Mama's plot at St. John's Cemetery,
Ozone Park, NY. 1946.

Me, Maria, Rose, and Vincenzina. March 1948.

My mother had an expression that said, "Those who spit in the sky, it will fall right back on their face." How true that is.

When Mama died, we all wore black clothes and hats with black veils. It was during the war and during that time, black stockings were hard to come by. We had to dye our stockings. My friends would say, "Jean, when your mother died, the world didn't stop living. The world still goes on." I hated them when they spoke like that. We didn't play the radio or sing. We were in deep mourning and went to the cemetery every Sunday. We led a very sheltered life. My cousins would come and visit us. They were so concerned about us. We loved them. I would grab them, hug them tightly and kiss them. They would playfully wriggle out of my arms, but they loved it.

Shortly after Mama's death, Uncle Dom had a heart attack. We were all concerned and begged my uncle to please take care of himself; we reminded him that we all expected him to take us down the aisle when we got married. He was delighted to know that because he didn't have any girls of his own to take down the aisle. We loved him so.

On this one occasion, Danny, Mrs. Mancino's son, came to visit us. It was months after Mama had died. As he was coming down the basement steps, he leaned over the banister and reached for the radio that was sitting on the top of the dining room server and turned it on. I asked him not to. He replied, "Come on Jean, your burying yourself. We're in America, and you're too young to be dressed in black for a year." So, for the sake of my sisters who were also worried about me, I let him leave the radio on. Danny was very much a part of our family. He was like a brother to Frankie. He and Frankie would go on family trips together.

I wasn't feeling well and seemed to be going into a deep depression, so I went to see the doctor. The doctor said, "Jean, you've got to take those black stockings, veil, and clothes off; or you'll end up in the hospital." My sisters begged me. They looked up to me as a mother because I had raised and taken care of them since I was eight years old. If a child of that age had to take care of three younger sisters nowadays—they would be all taken away.

So for the sake of my sisters, we all stopped wearing all of our black clothing. Because it was an Italian custom, Aunt Eleanor, whom I adored, felt insulted that I didn't respect my mother enough by wearing black for at least a year. I explained to her that it was not my idea but the doctor's orders to remove the black stockings and clothes as he was concerned that I was going to have a nervous breakdown. A few weeks later, Aunt Eleanor got an infection on her leg due to the dye of the stockings. The doctor told her not to wear them at all. When I saw Aunt Eleanor climbing the L transit steps while we were all on our way to work, I asked her, "Zia, was I supposed to wait until I got an infection or land in the hospital before I took off the black clothes?" She hugged and kissed me and said, "Forgive me, you're right."

My sisters and I didn't go anywhere; we didn't go to the movies or parties. Many friends of the family and neighbors came to our house, and we passed the time knitting and crocheting with them. Several months later, Maria, Rose, and Vincenzina went roller-skating. It was very nice. There was music and sometimes skaters would "dance" with a partner. Although they had to travel by bus a half hour away to get there, my sisters loved it. They made their own skating outfits and looked forward to it every week. In fact, later in time, each of my sisters met her future husband there. I rarely went. I liked to skate, too; but I went to choir rehearsal to sing, instead.

We continued to participate in the annual St. Joseph's Day memorial service that we had attended for years with Mama, who was devoted to St. Joseph. We began this tradition after my dad had died, when Mama moved to a basement apartment. Her neighbor's son was mistaken for someone else and was murdered. So she made a vow to have a memorial service at her house every year for her son on St. Joseph's Day. She transformed her basement into a little church. On one side was an altar with candles and flowers, a picture of her son, and a large statue of St. Joseph. In front of the altar, was a very large basket with blessed bread for St. Joseph. She would get twelve children from the orphanage and set a table for them representing the twelve apostles. Many people would come and bring food and also donate money for the orphanage. She'd feed everyone from soup to nuts. We would all sit around with the twelve kids and eat and talk. There were also a few men who, in the name of St. Joseph, would donate their time to play music with Italian instruments. She would also give out the blessed St. Joseph's bread to all her guests. We loved the bread. It was delicious. The texture was so fine and smooth.

We were at the annual St. Joseph's Day memorial service the year Mama died. From the midst of the crowd a woman turned to me and said, "You see that woman sitting at the other table? Your stepfather married her." She was a beautiful-looking woman, lovely dressed. I got up, and I went over to her. She looked up to me, and I said to her, "I understand you married Mr. Ventura." She nodded her head; and I said, "I do hope and wish you lots of luck, and I pray he treats you better than he treated my mother." She started to cry and took my hand and held it and said, "You are right. I should never have married him." I really felt sorry for her.

~

To this day, I don't understand how he could have married four times. He was ignorant, very unattractive, always had an angry look on his face, and his eyes bulged out. He had absolutely no charm. How he captivated all his wives is beyond me. Knowing that his punch caused my mother's death, I should hate him, but I don't. Had he been a good husband and respected Mama and treated her right, he would have been put on a pedestal. He didn't know how lucky he would have been. We would have been very happy if Mama had a good, decent, respectable mate and companion. She didn't have to die at the age of fifty. Had he been decent, maybe he would have taken us down the aisle on our wedding day.

I used to tell Uncle Frank, "You know, Uncle, because of you, I will never marry an Italian man." He would laugh and ask me why. I would say, "Because Italian men are jealous, suspicious, and are never appreciative." Maria, Rose, and Vincenzina all got married. They each wore a beautiful wedding dress, and I made the veil with a nice long train. We all used the same veil when we got married.

Each of my sisters' receptions was held at the American Legion a mile and a half from our home in Ozone Park. The hall was often used for catered events and weddings. At each of their receptions, we made sandwiches with all kinds of cold cuts and wrapped them nicely. There were three big, beautiful trays of cookies, pastries, and cream puffs; and also a tray of boxed candied almonds to give to the guests when they left. Soda, liquor, and wine were also served. We all decorated the hall. It was really beautiful. Maria married a Polish man, Rose married a Czechoslovakian, and Vincenzina married a German. Had they not given me their pay to manage, even after Mama died, each of them would not have been able to have such a big, beautiful wedding. Well, when I got married, guess whom I married—an Italian. As my mother said, "If you spit in the sky, you'll get it right back on your face." My sisters and I all got married at our church, St. Elizabeth's; but my reception was held in Larchmont, New York, next to Mamaroneck, where my husband lived.

Wow, I prayed to God that we all would have a better life than Mama had.

Biography

Jean Milone was born to Josephine Greco and Domenic Gagliardo on April 9, 1922, in New York City. The family moved to Ozone Park, New York, where her father died of tuberculosis when Jean was three-and-a-half years old. She had two younger sisters—Maria, then one-and-a-half; and newborn Rose. Her mother remarried to Vincenzo Nanfro in January 1929. He died six months later, in June 1929, while her mother was pregnant with her fourth child, Vincenzina, who was born in January 1930. Her mother remarried again in 1934. Married for five years to an abusive husband and stepfather, Jean's mother left him. As the oldest sibling, Jean had the responsibility of taking care of her three younger sisters. She completed the eighth grade and then attended high school for a short time before leaving school to work at the Treo Corset Company to help support her family. She went to night school in an attempt to complete her GED, but was unable to do so. Her mother was diagnosed with breast cancer in 1944 and died in 1946. Not until after her three younger sisters got married, did Jean marry Joseph Milone, in July 1951. She then moved to Mamaroneck, New York where she lives to this day. She has three children and four grandchildren.

In 1988, when Jean was sixty-six years old, determined to finish high school and get the diploma she never received, she completed a course at Westchester Community College in Valhalla, New York, where she received her GED. She retired at the age of eighty-one from Mamaroneck Avenue School in Mamaroneck, New York, where she worked as a teacher's aide for fourteen-and-a-half years. It was after her retirement that she began to write her mother's life story—a promise she had made to her mother more than sixty-six years earlier.

Jean experienced a young life of poverty, hardship, and abuse; yet she has led her life with compassion, perseverance, and tremendous enthusiasm.